Enlightened Risk Taking
A Guide to Strategic
Risk Management for Nonprofits

By George L. Head, Ph.D.
and Melanie L. Herman

Copyright © 2002
by the Nonprofit Risk Management Center

ISBN No. 1-893210-09-X

Nonprofit
Risk Management
Center

PUBLIC ENTITY RISK INSTITUTE
PERI

Nonprofit Risk Management Center

The Nonprofit Risk Management Center is dedicated to helping community-serving nonprofits conserve assets, prevent harm, and free up resources for mission-critical activities. The Center provides technical assistance on risk management, liability, and insurance matters; publishes easy-to-use written resources; designs and delivers workshops and conferences; and offers competitively priced consulting services.

The Center is an independent nonprofit organization that doesn't sell insurance or endorse specific insurance providers. For more information on the products and services available from the Center, call (202) 785-3891, or visit our Web site at **www.nonprofitrisk.org**.

Nonprofit Risk Management Center
1001 Connecticut Avenue, NW
Suite 410
Washington, DC 20036
(202) 785-3891
Fax (202) 296-0349
www.nonprofitrisk.org

Staff
Sheryl Augustine, *Customer Service Representative*
Amy Michelle DeBaets, *Director of Management Information Systems*
George L. Head, Ph.D., *Special Advisor*
Suzanne M. Hensell, *Director of Marketing and Education*
Melanie L. Herman, *Executive Director*
Barbara B. Oliver, *Director of Communications*
John C. Patterson, *Senior Program Director*

Public Entity Risk Institute

The Nonprofit Risk Management Center is grateful for the support of the Public Entity Risk Institute (PERI), which provided a generous grant to support the cost of publishing this book. PERI is a tax-exempt nonprofit whose mission is to serve public, private and nonprofit organizations as a dynamic, forward thinking resource for the practical enhancement of risk management. For more information on PERI, visit the organization's Web site: **www.riskinstitute.org**.

Acknowledgments

The Center is grateful to the following persons for their thoughtful comments and helpful suggestions on the draft of this publication:

Peggy M. Jackson, Ph.D., *Fogarty, Jackson & Associates*
Dennis M. Kirschbaum, ARM, *Hillel: The Foundation for Jewish Campus Life*
H. Felix Kloman, *Risk Management Reports*
Judith Nolan, *American Red Cross*
Linda P. Varnado, *American Red Cross*

Table of Contents

Introduction

"Who is wise? He who foresees what is coming."
— Jewish Proverb

N one of us knows exactly what tomorrow will bring. From experience, most of us — including most managers of nonprofit organizations — have good reasons to expect that tomorrow will be much like today. However, many events that we cannot now fully foresee may, occasionally and with little warning, make a nonprofit's tomorrow much different — much worse or much better — than it is today.

Thus, unpredictable events involving each of the four fundamental values within a nonprofit — its people, its property, its income and, perhaps most importantly, its reputation — may bring near disaster or great good fortune to a nonprofit depending on whether the threats or the opportunities outweigh the other.

■ For example, the *people* who work as employees or volunteers can be unexpected sources of loss or gain. *Loss* if, for example, a nonprofit's charismatic and talented executive director gives two weeks notice when the nonprofit has no clear successor available. *Gain* if, say, one of its high school volunteers comes up with a marvelous advertising slogan that memorably etches the nonprofit's mission into the public's mind.

■ With respect to *property*, a nonprofit may suffer a crippling unexpected *loss* if its headquarters burns to the ground one night; or may be surprised to *gain* funds beyond its supporters' dreams if a major oil or gold deposit is found beneath land recently bequeathed to it.

■ Regarding *income*, a nonprofit that sponsors youth recreation programs may face a substantial *loss* if, following a natural disaster, long-time donors shift their financial support to disaster relief through another organization. A nonprofit may *gain* huge financial success if the T-shirt it has chosen to market as a fundraiser is endorsed by a teen idol as something "all my true fans are wearing." Another surprising *income gain* might arise if a long-time volunteer inherits millions and makes an unexpected substantial donation to this nonprofit's previously meager endowment fund.

■ As for a nonprofit's *reputation*, great *loss* can come from any adverse news that makes regional or national headlines, such as reports of child abuse or misappropriation of assets by one of the nonprofit's employees. Great *gain* can come from positive behavior, such as an act of life-saving or patriotic heroism by one of the nonprofit's staff that draws network television or Internet attention.

All these events happen unexpectedly, and usually very suddenly. These events all arise from risk — that is, from a *measure of the possibility that the future may be surprisingly different from what we expect*. These surprises may bring good or bad results, generating threats of losses or presenting opportunities for gains. Each of these events holds within it threats of loss and opportunities for gain, which should be weighed before deciding whether or not to undertake the activity, program or event. For a nonprofit organization to fulfill its public service mission, its executives, other employees and volunteers must manage these risks effectively by countering or withstanding the *threats of loss* and recognizing and capitalizing on the *opportunities for gain* that are inherent in a less than fully predictable, and therefore risky, world.

This book explains how to strategically manage risk — how to take risks in enlightened ways that enable your nonprofit to fulfill its mission to the utmost in our less-than-fully-predictable world.

The Mission of This Book

This book explains how to strategically manage risk — how to take risks in enlightened ways that enable your nonprofit to fulfill its mission to the utmost in our less-than-fully-predictable world. This book is also about risk management — a process for planning, organizing, directing and controlling the assets and activities of any organization so that it can accomplish its mission by safeguarding against the losses, while seizing the opportunities for gain that risk generates.

This risk management process has five steps, previewed in Chapter 1. The steps are much the same for managing threats of loss from what we will call *downside risks* and opportunities for gain from *upside risks*. Most real-world situations actually present both upside and downside risks. So ideally, strategic risk management looks at the threat of things accidentally going wrong (the traditional use of risk management), as well as the potential for things to go right (the new twist or enlightened risk management proposed in this book).

Each chapter in this book aims to help you understand the risk management process and to apply this process to both the downside and the upside risks inherent in your nonprofit's activities, events and programs.

❑ Chapter 1 explores the nature of risk from both sides and explains some basic concepts that are key to managing risk effectively.

❑ Chapter 2 looks at what your nonprofit can lose from failing to manage risk well, and the types of opportunities for unanticipated gains that surprise events may bring to your nonprofit if you are alert to and ready to grasp them.

❑ Chapter 3 explains the five steps in the risk management process, illustrating how it works in both countering threats of loss and positioning your nonprofit to take advantage of opportunities for gain.

❑ Chapter 4 explores practical opportunities for nonprofits to use physical and managerial controls to reduce threats of accidental losses.

❑ Chapter 5 details the downside and upside risks arising from activities that are amplified in nonprofit organizations — such as working with volunteers, managing special events, and serving the needs of vulnerable populations.

As its title indicates, this is a book about *strategic risk management*. Strategic risk management, as we will be exploring it, differs significantly from both *general management* as one learns it in principles of management courses and from the *traditional risk management* that most safety, insurance and financial specialists practice.

The traditional safety and insurance perspective on risk management has been limited to only threats of loss — in fact, to just threats of *accidental* loss. In this traditional view, risk management does not deal with either opportunities for possible gain or with nonaccidental risks of loss, such as from poor business judgment or from errors in forecasting economic trends or weighing consumer preferences. In this traditional insurance-and-safety context, the most risk management could ever accomplish was *no losses from accidents*, so that an organization could, at best, *safely remain as it always has been.*

That men have forever taken huge risks, chancing enormous losses against equally large rewards, is a truism. It is a part of our nature. A recent television special on PBS focused on commercial fishermen in Scotland, Maine and Alaska. The sea extorts cruel penalties in the loss of life, boats and equipment, but it also supplies the successful with riches. The program reported that a crabber captain could earn as much as $150,000, and his crew members as much as $50,000, in three months of relentless toil in the Gulf of Alaska, enticing crews back to the vicious storms and the inevitable disappearances of men and ships for the possibility of the big payday. The losses are fearsome. Two boats, for example, capsized at the start of the voyage when they met a storm while overloaded with crab cages. It is a continuing reminder that risk decisions are always based on a personal assessment of both potential rewards and penalties. Even so, as this program reported, it too often appears to be a roll of the dice.

— H. Felix Kloman, *Risk Management Reports*, September 2002, reprinted with permission.

Our broader, *strategic risk management* view seeks to *1.) counter all losses*, both from accidents and from unfortunate business judgments and *2.) seize opportunities for gains* through organizational innovation and growth so that risk management, at its best, enables your nonprofit to *be all it can be.*

Stated in these be-all-it-can-be terms, strategic risk management may sound like it is identical to general management, but it is not. General management assumes that good planning will make plans come true, that good managerial controls will generate controlled outcomes. Thus, general management assumes that surprises, both good and bad ones, can largely be managed away.

As explored in this book, strategic risk management is based on quite a different premise. For a nonprofit or any other organization to achieve full potential for itself and those it seeks to serve, surprises must be anticipated, and preparations must be made, in order to turn aside or overcome the threats of bad surprises and embrace the opportunities the good surprises offer. This book's title, *Enlightened Risk Taking,* capsulizes this goal. The Center's purpose is not to avoid all risk, which is impossible. Instead, strategic risk management aims to take risk wisely: to eliminate or limit its negative effects so that you are better able to benefit from its positive effects. In doing so, strategic risk management seeks to maintain and enhance the confidence of an organization's "publics" (employees, supporters, service recipients, communities, donors and regulators) so that it can continue to fulfill its mission, now and in the future.

Chapter 1 turns, first, to the meaning of risk and of some closely related terms; second, to why we need to manage risk; and, third, to a preview of the general strategic risk management process for managing both threats from downside risks and opportunities from upside risks. Strategic risk management is the core concept of this book, the concept that the later chapters explain how to make a reality in your nonprofit organization.

The Several Surprising Sides of Risk

B uilding from a definition of "risk," this chapter describes the strategic risk management process and explains how this process helps your nonprofit fulfill its mission.

What Is Risk?

Risk is a measure of the possibility that the future may be surprisingly different from what we expect. This definition is important because it summarizes what risk — and, therefore, strategic risk management — is and what it is not.

Risk Is...

This definition suggests that risk is 1.) a measure (or estimate) of a possibility that 2.) may have some surprising dimensions.

A Possibility...

A risk is a measure (or estimate) of a possibility. Therefore, risk is neither an impossibility (which has no chance of happening) nor a certainty (which will definitely occur). Thus, risk is associated with events whose chances of happening are greater than zero but less than 100 percent. Where change occurs, risk arises.

By their very nature, nonprofit organizations and their supporters seek change — at least in the well-being of the constituents who are the focus of their nonprofit mission. Almost certainly, they also welcome change in the underlying conditions, such as poverty, ignorance or disease, which they strive to help these constituents conquer. For any community-serving nonprofit to succeed, its world must change; it cannot stand still, perfectly stable. Again by the world's very nature, it changes. This is fortunate because without change, there could be no progress. But with change, whether for better or for worse, there inevitably comes some instability, some unpredictability, some risk.

With Potentially Surprising Dimensions

Welcome or unwelcome change brings unpredictability. Here are three ways, or three dimensions, in which risk arises because the future may surprise your nonprofit.

1. Future events may be much worse or much better than you expect. Call this the *directional* — positive/negative — dimension.

2. Future events may happen much more often, or much less often, than you expect. Call this the *probability* — more/less likely — dimension.

3. Future events may generate bad or good results that are much larger, or much smaller, than we expect. Call this the *magnitude* or size — major/minor — dimension.

You may wish to summarize these three points by remembering that *risk is also the extent to which the future differs from our expectations.* When using this definition, remember that "extent" includes the 1.) direction, 2.) probability and 3.) magnitude of these differences between what we expect and what actually happens.

Consider how defining risk as *a measure of the possibility that the future may be surprisingly different from what we expect* helps in analyzing a typical downside risk and a typical upside risk for a nonprofit. Let the downside risk — long a concern of accident-centered traditional risk management — be that a particular nonprofit's employees or volunteers will suffer injuries while working for the nonprofit. Let the upside risk — a concern, along with downside risk, of strategic risk management — be that this same nonprofit will receive an unexpected large gift from a long-time supporter.

Both the worker-injury risk and the unexpected-donation risk present possibilities that the nonprofit's future will be surprisingly different from its present condition. Unexpected injuries may seriously impair the nonprofit's capacity to carry out its mission, while an unanticipated donation may greatly enhance this capacity. Each risk — each possibility for a markedly different future for this nonprofit — also has distinctive dimensions of direction, probability and magnitude. Worker injuries almost always produce only negative results, although it is possible that a nonprofit's efforts to adapt to the temporary absence of an injured worker may result in more efficient ways of doing things or showcase heretofore hidden talents of another employee. Unexpected donations typically produce only good results for a nonprofit, unless the nonprofit spends the unexpected "windfall" without regard to the public's perception of its appropriate use of the funds. Or in rare cases, widespread publicity about a large gift may lead to a decline in giving by the organization's core supporters who start wondering why they should give to this no longer "starving" nonprofit.

Therefore, what you expect the future to bring, and how you prepare for that future greatly affect the amount of risk confronting the organization you manage. Since *risk is a measure of the possibility that the future may be surprisingly different from what we expect*, the amount of risk each of you and your organizations face varies with 1.) what each of you expects the future to be and 2.) how much it takes to surprise you. If you have very specific expectations for your organization's future, and if you are unprepared for any other version of the future, so that any other version will greatly surprise you, then you and your organization face great risk.

For example, if you expect a year or a decade during which no employees will be injured on the job, or you have not prepared for any unusually large donations from unforeseen benefactors in that timeframe, then you and your nonprofit almost certainly will be surprised. You may be unable to respond appropriately when a key volunteer or officer suffers a work-related injury or a philanthropist asks what good uses your nonprofit will make of the $10 million that she wishes to donate. Surprised and unprepared, your nonprofit may have to restructure or suspend services to clients while adjusting for the absence of the injured key volunteer or officer. Further surprised and unprepared, with no clear, inspiring plan to use the offered $10 million, your nonprofit may lose this gift to another cause that this generous benefactor suddenly finds to be more deserving.

> **T**he rarest attribute in any society and culture, when things are generally going well, and peace and prosperity reign, and bellies are full of good food, and the sun shines and the rains fall appropriately, is to notice certain cracks in the edifice, some defects and problems, which if not attended to could in time undermine the happy ambiance and bring on distress and terror.
>
> — Norman F. Cantor, *In the Wake of the Plague: The Black Death & The World It Made*, 2001.

But if your expectations are less narrowly and more realistically focused, if you are prepared for a broader range of future outcomes, your organization faces less risk. With more enlightened expectations and heightened preparedness, you will not be as surprised when the disability of one or two of your nonprofit's key people requires you to restructure job assignments and take advantage of the staff's cross-training to maintain fairly normal operations until the disabled key people return or can be permanently replaced. Similarly, some thoughtful long-range planning and study of other successful nonprofits' growth should enable a fledgling nonprofit's managers to project its mission, funding options and alternative operating models to the point that the organization can constructively welcome an unexpected major patron.

Dealing effectively with a downside risk such as key person disability and an upside risk such as surprise donations illustrates both sides of strategic risk management.

Strategic risk management...

- Counters downside risks by:

  1. reducing the probability and magnitude of losses and

  2. stimulating recovery from these losses by rebuilding reputation and financial strength.

- Seizes upside risks by:

  1. searching for opportunities to more fully, more certainly and more efficiently achieve an organization's nonprofit goals; and

  2. developing plans to act on these opportunities when the future presents them.

For strategic risk management of both downside risks of loss and upside risks of gain, realistic expectations and thorough preparation are key. Together, gauging the range of potential future outcomes and getting ready for the full range of possibilities are the essential elements of strategic risk management — the essentials of empowering an organization to be all it can be in a less-than-fully-predictable world.

A Basis for Strategic Risk Management

Having pondered and defined "risk," we can now define "management" to give us a basis for characterizing "risk management" for strategic risk management purposes.

Risk is *a measure of the possibility that the future may be surprisingly different from what we expect.*

Management has many fine definitions in many excellent books. A good consensus definition, describing management as a process within an organization, is that *management is using an organization's resources and activities to achieve some objective.* As we have seen, the central objective of strategic risk management is to counter unforeseen losses and to seize unexpected opportunities so that the organization can strive to achieve its full potential in a less-than-fully-predictable world.

Putting all these ideas together, *strategic risk management* may be defined as *using an organization's resources and activities to counter potential losses and seize potential gains.*

While accurately embracing many concepts, this definition may still be a little academic. If you find that the definition is too academic, just think of *strategic risk management* as *running a nonprofit as best you can so that it may fulfill its mission to the fullest in an uncertain future*. Making these few words a real working part of your daily management philosophy will make you a better strategic risk manager for your nonprofit.

Risk Relates to, But Is Not ...

Unlike *risk*, which has a rather special meaning in strategic risk management, most of the other words frequently used in this field mean much the same in strategic risk management as they mean in everyday language. However, there are three terms — *uncertainty*, *cause of loss* and *danger* — that have particular meanings for insurance and safety professionals working in an accidental-loss, downside-risk context. Oddly, the *concepts* that these three terms express for downside risks are helpful in strategic risk management of *both* downside and upside risks, so we need to look at their downside meanings and, where needed, find some upside terms for the underlying concepts.

Uncertainty

In its simplest terms, *uncertainty* means lack of knowledge or belief about something. Something about which we lack knowledge or firm belief is uncertain. In this sense, and putting aside any religious beliefs about life after death, all the future is uncertain for everyone and every organization.

Beyond this basic meaning, *uncertainty* can refer to the entire atmosphere within which we operate. In the physical world, an event is uncertain if the forces that may cause or prevent that event are not yet fully operative. For example, whether a specific building will burn tonight (a downside risk) or whether a foundation will approve your nonprofit's application for a major grant before the weekend (an upside risk) are — until tomorrow or the weekend — both uncertain events in the real world. Until each of these two events do or do not happen at the specified time, these possible events have physical-world, or objective, uncertainty.

Uncertainty is important to strategic risk management because nonprofit managers must make decisions without full knowledge of all the factors that affect a decision. To make better decisions that are more likely to fulfill their nonprofits' missions, managers should increase their knowledge, thus reducing uncertainty. Sometimes, this increased knowledge involves historical or current trends. At other times, only extremely current knowledge can reduce uncertainty. Thus, to better judge whether your headquarters burned last night, it is useful to know whether it was the police or the vandals who were patrolling the neighborhood last night, whether the automatic fire-suppression sprinkler system was operational, and whether someone forgot to turn off the office coffeepot. Being reassured on all these points might quiet your fiery nightmares, reducing your subjective uncertainty. But you will never really know until you check your nonprofit's headquarters in the morning.

Cause of Loss

In traditional risk management centered on accidental losses, *a cause of loss is the force that most directly or most predominantly brings about a loss.* For fire losses, fire is the cause of loss, regardless of how the fire starts, and regardless of whether the fire damages an organization's property, shuts the organization down for a time and causes loss of income, or injures the organization's employees or service recipients. Such natural causes of loss as wind or earthquake, human causes of loss such as criminal acts, or economic causes of loss such as recession or foreign currency devaluation can bring about similar losses. For liability losses, the cause of loss is the filing of a claim against an organization because — regardless of the merits of the claim — the filing forces the organization to divert some of its financial or managerial resources to resisting the claim, either directly or through its liability insurer.

As a counterpart, the direct, predominant cause of the gain in upside risks is management insight. This insight may involve actual innovation, or it may involve creative adaptations of others' ideas or practices. To illustrate, management insight in the form of *innovation* could be developing a new, terrifically effective method to teach illiterate Americans to read and write English. While management insight in the form of *recognition* could be realizing that this same method could be used to teach English or other languages very quickly and at low cost to virtually all preschoolers in the United States. Management insight may also lead the investment committee of a nonprofit to invest surplus funds or endowment resources in a way that enables the nonprofit to generate gain beyond expectation. Management insight, whether through innovation or new application of known methods, often generates surprising new values.

Small Nonprofits

Risk management is important for small nonprofits. Why? Because small organizations often have less resources to draw on when things turn out differently than they expect. And insurance and other risk financing tools may not be available due to the nonprofit organization's meager financial resources. But every organization, from the smallest to the largest, can and should take time to look into the future and predict both downside and upside risks. And as this book will illustrate, measures to address risk should be practical and within the reach of the organization. It is up to every nonprofit to select the strategies and approaches that it can afford and reasonably accomplish.

Danger

In accident-centered traditional risk management, a *danger is an action or a condition that tends to increase the probability or the magnitude of a loss.* For example, with fire, the smoking of cigarettes is a danger that raises the probability of fire damage to other property, and storage of large quantities of flammable liquids is a danger that increases the probable severity of any fire losses. For liability losses (where the bringing of a legal claim is the cause of loss), negligent or unlawful conduct by an organization is a danger, because such conduct makes it more likely that a claim will be filed against the organization. Moreover, the more harmful or shocking the conduct, the larger the claim (and perhaps the ultimate settlement or verdict) may be.

For upside risks, the concept that corresponds to a danger is an act or condition that makes a *gain*, not a loss, larger or more likely. Here, the term *safeguard* is appropriate because it signifies protection of a potential or actual gain. Furthermore, where an ongoing activity or situation with an upside risk also presents a possible downside risk, the concept of a safeguard suggests limiting the downside risk. For example, a nonprofit clinic may have a great opportunity to extend its outreach by affiliating with, and becoming a rent-paying tenant within, a major for-profit hospital in another part of the same city where this nonprofit has been renting separate, less desirable space. For its part, the hospital views an alliance with this nonprofit as a cost-effective way to extend its services and become more competitive with other hospitals in the city.

However, at least two downside risks of potential loss for the nonprofit are inherent in this new affiliation:

1. many members of the nonprofit's client base may not know of the move to, or may be reluctant to visit, the new upscale hospital facility, which requires a long bus ride from where they live; and,

2. future increases in the rent the nonprofit must pay the hospital, or even fixed rent payments if the nonprofit's level of activity decreases, may jeopardize the nonprofit's financial strength.

As safeguards of the increased success the nonprofit hopes this move to the hospital will achieve, its contract with the hospital may well include:

1. an ongoing joint publicity campaign in which the nonprofit and the hospital continue to alert the public to the community-wide benefits of their affiliation; and

2. a rent-adjustment formula that recognizes the financial needs of both the nonprofit tenant and the hospital landlord under a wide range of possible financial futures for both affiliated parties.

Why Manage Risk?

Risk may bring either downside losses or upside gains in the uncertain future. Therefore, the most straightforward answer to the question, "Why manage risk?" is *We manage risk to reduce potential losses and to increase potential gains.* At this level, strategic risk management of both downside and upside surprises from what we expect is no more than using informed common sense to make the most of a less-than-fully-predictable future. But to make strategic risk management a daily reality for your nonprofit, you need more concrete operational goals. Five good reasons for a nonprofit to manage risk are:

1. to counter losses,

2. to seize opportunities,

3. to reduce uncertainty,

4. to be a good citizen, and

5. to fulfill a community-serving mission.

These five basic operational goals for strategic management are the foundation for adopting a strategic risk management plan for your nonprofit. Together they enhance public confidence in the organization, assuring its future value to the community.

To Counter Losses

In traditional risk management, where accidental losses are the sole focus of attention, countering these losses is the essence of risk management. Countering accidental losses involves both:

■ reducing the probability, magnitude or unpredictability of accidental losses; and

■ financing recovery from accidental losses that cannot be prevented.

As will be detailed in Chapter 4, the first group of traditional risk management techniques for reducing accidental losses involves either avoiding or modifying the activities that may generate accidental losses. The second group of techniques uses either the retention of the financial burden of these losses within the nonprofit organization, or the sharing of this burden with other organizations beyond the specific nonprofit.

For example, a nonprofit that provides recreational opportunities to youth is exposed to many property and liability losses from roadway accidents if it chooses to transport these children to and from its facilities each day. To reduce these accidents, the nonprofit may decide not to provide transportation for these youth (*avoidance*). Alternatively, the nonprofit may continue transporting children but only after making sure that its drivers are well trained, the vehicles are well maintained, and the routes traveled are the safest possible (three examples of *modifying* activities to lessen loss exposures).

To pay for losses from those roadway accidents that may strike the nonprofit, the nonprofit may use its own funds (*retention*), or contract with a separate bus company for this transportation (in effect, *sharing* the financial burden of these accidents). Remember these losses could be

We Manage Risk to...

■ counter losses

■ seize opportunities

■ reduce uncertainty

■ be a good citizen

■ fulfill our mission

from groundless liability claims brought against the nonprofit merely because the nonprofit sponsored the recreation to which children were being transported in their parents' or friends' personal vehicles. Another way the nonprofit could share the costs of these accidents is to buy physical damage and liability insurance for its own buses. Under such insurance, the insurer would pay for the nonprofit's property and liability losses that fall within the scope of this insurance, leaving the insured nonprofit to pay for only those elements of its losses that go beyond the limits of this coverage.

To Seize Opportunities

When management insights let you see opportunities for gain or other progress, whether through your own innovation or the ability to recognize possibilities that others have overlooked, strategic risk management better enables you to seize these opportunities. While virtually nothing can assure total success in an uncertain future, you will see later in this chapter that strategic risk management increases your chances of success by:

1. creating opportunities by innovating within your organization or by adapting others' innovations to your purposes;

2. evaluating opportunities as they develop;

3. remaining ready to act on those opportunities that appear promising;

4. introducing new operating procedures that grasp chosen opportunities in timely ways and, if they prove successful, making these new operating procedures part of the organization's routine activities; and

5. assessing over time whether seizing each chosen opportunity has benefited the organization and those whom it serves.

To illustrate, consider the nonprofit clinic, when it was occupying its separate facility before affiliating with and moving to the for-profit hospital. To responsibly take advantage of the opportunity that this move offered, this nonprofit's management had to:

1. be consciously aware of, and open to, the possibility that a working relationship with some other health-care organization might help the nonprofit fulfill its mission more effectively.

2. be watchful for other kindred health-care facilities with which it might join forces and weigh the potential advantages and disadvantages to the nonprofit of affiliating with each potential partner health-care facility.

3. have a general standby physical, financial and public relations moving plan ready for whenever a really promising opportunity to affiliate arose.

4. adapt its daily routines to the move, so that it could serve its clients without significant interruption during, immediately after, and in the months following its move to the hospital.

5. assess periodically whether this affiliation and relocation continue to be in its and its clients' best interests — or whether the clinic should again seek a new physical and organizational home.

Good strategic risk management enables the individual managers and board members of a nonprofit to make the most of an unpredictable world.

For example, recall that before the move, the nonprofit was concerned that its client population might not follow it to its new location, and that its new rent payments might prove too burdensome. In this final evaluating and monitoring step of the strategic risk management process, the nonprofit's managers would continue to revisit these concerns.

The five steps of this strategic risk management process applied here to the upside opportunity risks of this nonprofit's affiliation are just as important when applied to its downside threats of loss associated with these changes. For example, threats of accidental loss from damage to the nonprofit's equipment during the actual move, and threats of business losses if its client base drifts away rather than commuting all the way to the new hospital location. We will detail this universal strategic risk management process later in this chapter and in the chapters that follow.

To Reduce Uncertainty

Another reason to manage risk is to reduce uncertainty in the minds of key stakeholders, both in the sense of the unpredictability of future events in the real world and in the sense of a troubled, doubtful state of mind. In both these senses, uncertainty is reduced by gathering more data for making better predictions and by anticipating and preparing for a wider range of outcomes.

Again in both these senses, reduced uncertainty brings two major benefits to a nonprofit. First, more accurate forecasts of the future make better decisions possible. Managers are better able to make decisions that more effectively advance the nonprofit's mission, or — if they do make a wrong decision — are better prepared to take prompt corrective action. Second, reduced psychological uncertainty among managers makes them more confident in moving forward, more optimistic in making the changes that the realization of their mission requires, less agonized by paralyzing doubts, and able to sleep restfully at night. Just as it does for their organizations, good strategic risk management enables the individual managers and board members of a nonprofit to make the most of an unpredictable world.

To Be a Good Citizen

Organizations are good citizens when they act according to accepted standards. These standards may be legal, ethical or rooted in a commitment to a better world.

As a reason for managing risk for any nonprofit, being a good citizen involves both obeying the law and behaving ethically. For any organization, activities that fulfill both legal and ethical requirements reduce the probability that it will be sued and — particularly important for nonprofit organizations — foster a favorable public image for the organization. Thus, acting as a good citizen both tends to insulate an organization from liability losses (a downside risk) and opens opportunities for an organization to gain positive public support (an upside risk).

Ideally, legal standards and ethical standards for an organization call for the same activities: What is legal is ethical, and what is ethical is also legal. However this is not always the case — a nonprofit's view of ethical conduct with respect to some risks may exceed, or may fall short of, legal requirements. For example, a nonprofit may encourage its members or staff to engage in civil disobedience to protest government action. A nonprofit whose mission relates to employee safety may believe that current federal workplace ergonomic standards are entirely inadequate. For its own employees, this second nonprofit may wish to follow ergonomic practices that exceed governmental standards.

The management of each nonprofit organization must, at a minimum, obey the law in order to reduce its liability losses. Failing to meet legal standards may expose the organization and its staff and board members to needless lawsuits, be poor stewardship of the nonprofit's resources, and constitute a breach of the duties that the employees and trustees of a nonprofit owe to it. For example, failing to meet building or sanitation codes, allowing employees to use the nonprofit's vehicles in ways that violate traffic codes, or serving food or drink in ways that endanger public health and safety would violate not only the law but the public trust. Where a nonprofit's mission calls for conduct that exceeds some legal standard, its management must decide whether following the law is sufficient or whether, instead, it should strive for the higher standard that its vision of a better world seeks. Or in the case of an organization promoting civil disobedience, the nonprofit must decide if the benefits of its failure to operate within the law outweigh the costs of doing so.

These concerns arise when a nonprofit's mission calls for challenging and ultimately changing particular laws to which the nonprofit and its supporters conscientiously object. For instance, an animal-rights nonprofit may object to — and may try to interfere physically with — the manufacturing and marketing activities of a beef or pork producer that the nonprofit believes is unnecessarily cruel in slaughtering its livestock, even though its killing technique arguably is within the law. To stop this cruelty and eventually tighten the law, this nonprofit may choose to picket this meat producer's facilities, block its delivery trucks, or conduct informational leaflet campaigns in stores where this producer's meats are sold. Invoking the spirit of early American patriots, the management of this nonprofit may think of these actions as *civil disobedience* in service of the public good. In conducting these protests, however, the managers of this nonprofit need to avoid trespassing on this meat producer's property, damaging its vehicles, injuring its employees, interfering unduly with the operation of any wholesale or retail meat market, or injuring a buyer in any such market. Any such wrongful acts could expose the nonprofit and any of its personnel who were directly involved to liability for intentional or reckless, conceivably criminal, harm to others.

To Fulfill a Community-Serving Mission

Nonprofit organizations perform many functions in the public interest that neither governments nor profit-seeking firms could or would wish to perform. In exchange for these community-serving efforts, federal and state governments grant nonprofit organizations some significant tax, regulatory and other advantages that others do not enjoy. In return, these governments expect nonprofit organizations to devote their resources as effectively as possible to the purposes expressed in their mission statement.

Strategic risk management strives to nourish a nonprofit's resources by empowering it to seize opportunities to grow toward greater mission fulfillment. Nonprofits cannot avoid risks. Changing the world or our next-door neighbors' tomorrow for the better requires taking risks in enlightened ways.

Strategic risk management is an essential part of this public trust to make the most effective use of your nonprofit's resources for community service. On the one hand, strategic risk management aims to prevent these resources from being needlessly sacrificed to accidental losses caused by downside risks. On the other, strategic risk management strives to nourish a nonprofit's resources by empowering it to seize opportunities to grow toward greater mission fulfillment. Nonprofits cannot avoid risks. Changing the world or our next-door neighbors' tomorrow for the better requires taking risks in enlightened ways. It requires *Enlightened Risk Taking*.

As you read the pages that follow and consider how to best implement the recommendations within your nonprofit, bear in mind that most nonprofits are experienced risk takers. They recognize that without taking bold risks they have no hope of reaching hard-to-serve client populations, recruiting armies of volunteers, or raising enough money to meet operating expenses. Nonprofits welcome the challenges associated with meeting compelling community needs.

The General Risk Management Process

Strategic risk management helps you to make the best decisions possible for your nonprofit as it strives to succeed in an inherently unpredictable future. This success requires that your nonprofit both reduce its accidental losses and increase its gains from upside risks that arise from mission-related opportunities.

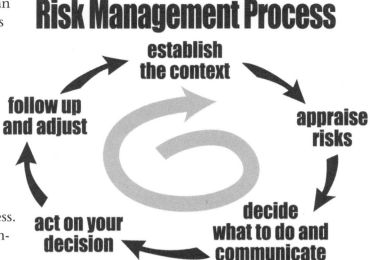

Risk Management Process

establish the context → appraise risks → decide what to do and communicate → act on your decision → follow up and adjust

For both downside threats of accidental losses and upside opportunities for mission gains, strategic risk management rests on one five-step, decision-making process. This process is similar to the decision-making process that *traditional* risk management employs in dealing with only the downside risks of accidental losses, but the concepts and terminology of *strategic* risk management are broader and more inclusive. These five steps are:

1. Establish the context.

2. Appraise risks.

3. Decide what to do and communicate your decision.

4. Act on your decision.

5. Follow up and adjust.

PHASE 1

Risk Analysis

RISK IDENTIFICATION, EVALUATION AND MEASUREMENT

PHASE 2

Risk Response

RISK CONTROL, FINANCING AND COMMUNICATION

Another way to look at the process is to group its steps into two phases: Phase I is Risk Analysis, which encompasses risk identification, evaluation and measurement. Phase II, Risk Response, entails risk control, financing and communication.

We will explore and apply this process throughout the rest of this book, especially in Chapter 3 which details these five steps and charts their components. To get a sense of how this process works, this chapter sketches how the management of the nonprofit that provides maternal and prenatal advice and health care to disadvantaged women might apply strategic risk management to:

1. its downside risk of liability arising out of unfavorable medical outcomes for its clients and

2. its upside risk of increased revenue from affiliating with the general hospital in the same city.

Step 1
Establish the Context

For risks to arise, it must be possible for future events to differ significantly from what we expect. The context of strategic risk management includes the setting, the surroundings, and the notion of what is *routinely normal* and of what we want the future to be like. The context establishes the background of expectations against which surprises may happen and must be strategically managed.

As Chapter 3 elaborates, the elements of the context within which a nonprofit organization must make strategic risk management decisions include the organization's:

❑ objectives,

❑ resources,

❑ attitude toward risk,

❑ constraints,

❑ management structure and style, and

❑ the environment — particularly the economic, regulatory and historical setting — in which it operates now and forecasts for the future.

For example, with respect to liability claims (downside risks) related to its clients' medical care, important parts of the context for making strategic risk management decisions would include the specific kinds of medical advice and services this nonprofit provides, the size and expertise of its professional staff, the number and types of claims it considers *normal*, and its objectives for controlling future claims costs. Similarly, for the upside opportunities for increased income from hospital affiliation, the context in which this nonprofit's management would make decisions about affiliating would include the general economic environment of the city where both organizations are located, as well as the financial strength, management styles and long-term objectives of each of them.

Step 2
Appraise Risks

Appraising risks is a general term for estimating, evaluating, judging and/or setting priorities among ways in which the future may be surprisingly different from what we expect it to be for our nonprofit. Appraising risks requires:

❑ looking at how the values — people, property, income and reputation — of a nonprofit may unexpectedly change (decrease or increase) in the future;

❑ the probability, magnitude and predictability of these changes; and

❑ the effect of these changes on the nonprofit's mission.

To assess the maternal health-care nonprofit's medical liability claim (downside) risk, its management would consider:

❑ how such claims could adversely effect its personnel, income and other resources;

❑ the reasonably likely ranges of numbers and amounts of such claims in the next one, five, and perhaps 10 years, and how predictable these claims may or may not be; and

❑ the effect that an increase or decrease would have on the continuing ability of this nonprofit to serve its clientele.

As for the upside risk from possibly affiliating with the general hospital, a risk assessment would focus on whether — and if so how much — making this change would enhance (perhaps detract from) the nonprofit's staff, income from grants and from clients, operating expenses, reputation, and community-serving capability.

Step 3
Decide What to Do and Communicate Your Decision

In selecting techniques for dealing with either downside threats of loss or upside opportunities for gain, one looks methodically at *all* the available risk management techniques and then most likely chooses some combination of techniques that most cost-effectively contributes to the organization's goals. For a nonprofit, the principal goal is to maintain public confidence. Additional goals relate to units of service provided or numbers of clients served within a given budget.

For all types of organizations, however, the types of risk management techniques from which to choose, or which to combine in the most cost-effective mix, are much the same. For downside risks of accidental loss, the choices are among techniques for controlling losses and techniques for paying for any losses that still occur. Thus, for liability claims arising from adverse medical outcomes, this nonprofit could control losses by declining to serve some types of high-risk applicants or could modify its post-treatment follow-up procedures to identify more quickly clients who are not faring well. To finance liability claims it cannot prevent, this nonprofit could purchase malpractice liability insurance, and then, at the discretion of the nonprofit's executive director, pay very minor claims out of a special internal fund.

For upside risks, the most appropriate techniques are those that most reliably and cost-effectively increase the probability and size of the potential gains from pursuing a mission-based opportunity while limiting the potential loss from choosing the wrong opportunity or from bungling what otherwise would have been a good opportunity. These techniques should be used in sequence. The techniques involve:

❑ exercising managerial insight to recognize or create favorable opportunities;

❑ remaining ready with contingency plans to seize opportunities quickly when they arise;

❑ acting on these plans; and

❑ evaluating the results during, immediately after taking action, and in the months and years that follow.

This nonprofit could take each of these steps, starting with a general readiness to consider potentially advantageous affiliations with kindred organizations.

Step 4
Act on Your Decision

Once a particular risk management decision has been made — for example, "Let's buy medical malpractice insurance to protect us against liability claims," or "Let's affiliate with a hospital in the city for the growth opportunities it offers and the possibility of free rent" — it is tempting to relax, thinking that the strategic risk management of these matters is basically finished. But it is not. The real work of risk management is just beginning. And the effectiveness of tactical responses depends on the skills of those assigned to the work.

Having selected any given risk management technique to counter a given threat of loss or to seize a given opportunity for gain, a nonprofit's managers must make two further types of decisions to implement that technique:

1. *technical decisions* relating to the intricacies of the chosen technique itself and

2. *administrative decisions* relating to the actions the personnel within the nonprofit must take to put the chosen technique into practice.

The technical decisions require specialized expertise, often from outside the nonprofit; the administrative decisions call for detailed knowledge of the particular nonprofit's internal workings.

As an example, suppose the nonprofit clinic decides to protect itself against medical liability claims by screening out new applicants for care who had certain high-risk medical characteristics and, instead, refer them to a specialized hospital or other facility. Two technical decisions it then has to make are:

1. What are the high-risk criteria that will disqualify an applicant?

2. To what other facilities will these applicants be referred?

Two related administrative decisions are:

1. How should the decision to reject an applicant be communicated, and what documents should be generated in such cases?

2. Should every professional member of the nonprofit's staff or only selected staff, be trained and authorized to reject such applicants?

Following on the initial decision to obtain medical liability insurance for this nonprofit, two technical decisions are:

1. How much insurance to purchase; and

2. From which insurer.

Individual members of the nonprofit's board may or may not wish to become involved in these decisions, and current conditions in the market for medical liability insurance may or may not offer many options. As for internal administrative decisions pertaining to such insurance, the nonprofit's management would need to:

❑   select which of its employees (and perhaps which volunteers) would be covered by this insurance and,

❑   train, perhaps with guidance from its insurance agent or broker, all its personnel to avoid conduct that, according to the insurance policy wording, could suspend or terminate coverage.

After opting to seek growth opportunities by affiliating with a hospital in the same city, this nonprofit also would face some technical and managerial decisions. One technical decision would relate to the characteristics a hospital must have before the nonprofit would even consider joining with it; another would focus on the boundaries of the range of financial arrangements that the nonprofit could make with any hospital without endangering its nonprofit status. Administratively, the nonprofit's management would have to decide, as it progressed in its negotiations and planning for the new affiliation, when and in what detail to tell its current employees, volunteers and clients about the impending changes. Losing the participation and allegiance of any of these groups could be a significant potential loss arising from this essentially upside opportunity.

Step 5
Follow up and Adjust

The preceding four steps in strategic risk management select and put into place one or more risk management techniques for each of the downside threats of loss and upside opportunities of gain that the managers of a nonprofit have identified as critical to the nonprofit's mission. By implementing these four steps, the nonprofit's leadership has created a risk management program. The fifth and final step in strategic risk management aims to verify that this resulting overall risk management program has been correct in producing the expected results for the nonprofit (*following up*), and remains flexible so that it corrects for shortcomings and adjusts to changing conditions (*adjusting*). Risks do not remain static; they change continually.

As Chapter 3 will explain further, monitoring an existing risk management program entails setting standards for risk management performance, measuring actual results against these standards and improving substandard performance. Adjusting a risk management program requires remaining alert to changes in:

1. any of the factors that shape a strategic risk management program — for example, changes in the nature, probability or magnitude of any threats of loss or opportunities for gains;

2. the availability or costs of any of the techniques for dealing with these threats or opportunities; and

3. a nonprofit's technological, economic or regulatory environment.

Modifying a risk management program then requires reconsidering the resulting changes in the downside and upside risks that the nonprofit faces and re-evaluating each of the previously selected risk management techniques to see if they remain appropriate in the new strategic risk environment. In doing so, your nonprofit should also seek to uncover new risks.

Make Changes as You Go

Modifying a risk management program includes re-evaluating each of the previously selected risk management techniques to see if it remains appropriate in the new strategic risk environment. In doing so, your nonprofit should also seek to uncover new risks.

Consider three examples of this monitoring/modifying step in strategic risk management involving the same maternity/neonatal medical nonprofit. In the first example, assume that a very safe and effective medication becomes available to treat what has been a very high-risk condition among pregnant women. Therefore, the nonprofit can relax its criterion for screening out applicants with this condition and referring them to a specialized facility, *provided the nonprofit can be sure that these applicants are taking, and continue to take the new medication.* Therefore, if it drops this screening criterion, the nonprofit must initiate a test to verify that these women continue their medication — a case of both monitoring and modifying the nonprofit's risk management measures in response to a changed risk environment.

In the second example, assume this nonprofit learns that the premium for its medical liability insurance is going to increase at its next renewal in a few months. A few weeks before this renewal, the nonprofit receives an unrestricted $100,000 bequest. The nonprofit's board may well consider whether to increase its retention of smaller medical liability claims by some amount up to $100,000 and conservatively invest the bequest in anticipation of claims within the increased retention. Increasing its retention will save insurance premium dollars, and the earnings from the newly invested funds will increase the nonprofit's overall revenues. As these insurance premiums fluctuate, and the rate of return the nonprofit can safely earn on its invested funds also varies over time, the finance committee or the entire board of this nonprofit may wish to adjust its retention/insurance mix of sources for paying medical liability claims.

Risk Management Process

establish
the context

appraise
risks

decide
what to do and
communicate

act on your
decision

follow up
and adjust

As a third example, this nonprofit's management may want to be especially cautious as it moves forward with its affiliation with the general hospital. Even after moving to its new facilities there, the nonprofit may find that its long-time employees and clients, who initially said they would remain with the organization, begin to drift away. Or the nonprofit's staff may find unexpected incompatibilities and administrative complications in trying to fit into the hospital environment. For its part, the hospital may encounter similar difficulties trying to accommodate its new nonprofit tenant. Therefore, as a risk management measure, they may both wish to include in their rental contract provisions for:

■ either party to terminate the lease with six months notice; and

■ a procedure for mediating or arbitrating any difficulties that the parties themselves cannot satisfactorily resolve.

The final step in strategic risk management basically returns the decision-making process to its beginning:

1. establishing the now-current environment;

2. appraising the perhaps-altered threats of loss and opportunities for gain;

3. examining which risk management techniques remain appropriate and which need minor or major changes; and

4. implementing the still appropriate and revised techniques.

The strategic risk management process never ends.

Summary

In Chapter 1 we saw that strategic risk management is something quite *new* — new because it copes simultaneously with threats of accidental losses and opportunities for gains — all from surprising, unexpected events. Traditional risk management has focused on the downside risks of accidental loss. *Strategic* risk management aims to enhance a nonprofit's opportunities for gain. *Traditional* risk management tries to *keep* a nonprofit *safe; strategic* risk management strives to *safely nurture* an organization to its fullest.

CHAPTER 2

Appraising Potential Surprises
What We Can Lose or Gain

In Chapter 2, we take another view of strategic risk management using the profession of teaching as a metaphor. Teaching is in many respects about nurturing — keeping children secure from harm, and enabling children to grow to their greatest potential.

Teachers seek these dual goals of safety and growth in the face of uncertainties. Some of these uncertainties may arise from such downside threats as lack of resources or family strife that may endanger children. Other uncertainties present upside risks. A teacher may be blessed with a large number of bright and eager students in one year's class, or a new text or approach for teaching history may inspire remarkable learning. Teachers are strategic risk managers — nurturing the resources entrusted to them by promoting both the safety and development of students.

Managers of nonprofits also should be strategic risk managers by nurturing — both protecting and developing in the face of uncertainty — the community-serving resources entrusted to them and to their organizations. The valued assets that need to be protected and nurtured are widely recognized within the nonprofit community. They are people, property, income and reputation. This chapter examines:

1. typical examples of the assets within a nonprofit;

2. the threats of accidental losses that may cause the loss of these assets; and

3. the types of opportunities through which, with the insight to innovate and to adapt, a nonprofit's managers may increase an organization's future assets to more effectively carry out its mission.

This chapter concentrates on the second step in the general strategic risk management process:

❑ Appraise both downside and upside risks.

(Recall from Chapter 1 that a *risk is a measure of the possibility that the future may be surprisingly different* — much worse or much better — *from what we expect*.) Later chapters will explore the remaining three steps in strategic risk management for nonprofits.

Appraising Mission-Critical Values

As we said, four broad classes of assets have value and are essential to the success of a community-serving nonprofit. These asset classes are 1.) people, 2.) property, 3.) income and 4.) reputation. The first three asset classes are tangible, while the fourth is intangible. While any two nonprofits may differ in the specifics of these broad classes and in the threats and opportunities most crucial to each nonprofit, every appraisal of a nonprofit's strategic risk management situation should begin with an inventory of these four classes of assets.

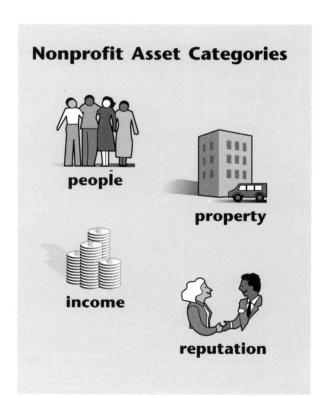

Nonprofit Asset Categories

people

property

income

reputation

Inventory is an especially key word throughout the chapter. Even though virtually every nonprofit possesses (and needs to protect and to nourish) assets in each of these four classes, no two nonprofits have exactly the same mix of assets. As we survey the kinds of people, property, income and reputational assets that characterize most nonprofits, inventory your own. Take a mental stroll through your nonprofit's facility, organization chart, client groups and perhaps operations manual and note what specific people, property, income-generating activities and reputation are of value to you.

We will start by just looking at the mission-related value of assets, asking "How would our ability to carry out our mission be impaired if this particular person (or item or property/legal right, or income-generating process, or group that supports us) were completely gone or were greatly reduced?" If the answer is "We would really have trouble fulfilling our mission," you have identified a mission-critical asset. If the answer is "Not that much," then that asset is probably not crucial. If you answer, "It would not make any difference at all," then perhaps supporting that person, property or process is not a good use of your nonprofit's resources. This chapter will suggest some general answers to this question about inventorying critical assets, but you should try to fill in some specifics for your particular nonprofit.

Once you have identified mission-critical assets, you will take these same assets (hopefully as you have tailored them for your nonprofit) and ask, "What surprising events could eliminate or greatly reduce these values?" Your answers to this question will highlight some key downside risks of accidental loss. For these downside threats of loss, you will want to consider "How often?" "How bad?" and "How predictable?" so that you can begin to gauge the frequency, magnitude and uncertainty of these downside risks.

Then turn to upside risks, unexpected opportunities for gain, and — for the same inventory of mission-critical assets — ask, "What surprising, unanticipated events could greatly increase the assets' values?" And again, how likely are these events, what is the potential size (magnitude) of these gains, and how predictable are these events? Finally, what kinds of managerial insights — *innovations* or *recognition of possibilities for progress* that others have missed — will position your nonprofit to seize these opportunities when they come across your path?

Once you have the basic inventory of critical values and turn to the downside and upside risks from surprising events, you will focus on truly unanticipated events, not routine or inevitable events. Examples of the difference follow. Two events that can remove a nonprofit's officers or employees are illness or retirement. But in any well-managed organization, routine illnesses and retirements are anticipated; they are not risks. In contrast, the death of all three of a nonprofit's most senior executives in the same airplane crash is a risk. On the upside, the steady growth of a nonprofit's income because its donors are increasing in number or wealth is not an upside risk. A bequest of 1,000 acres in the Amazon Basin of South America is an upside risk for *most* nonprofits headquartered in the United States. An upside risk for an organization whose mission focuses on fighting a particular disease is the sudden discovery of a medicine that definitely cures that disease. The risk escalates if the discoverer of the cure is a very prominent medical researcher who helped found the nonprofit.

People

The success of most nonprofits depends upon the efforts, support or at least the cooperative approval of five groups of people:

❑ the nonprofit's board whose dedication and vision energize its efforts;

❑ the employees, volunteers, and independent contractors who labor for the nonprofit;

❏ the service recipients, whose improved well-being is the reason for the nonprofit's continued existence;

❏ major donors of money or property to the nonprofit; and

❏ the public, whose support for (or at least tolerance of) the nonprofit's mission is crucial to its financial and political survival.

Within each of these five groups, any one individual's value to a given nonprofit is particularly great when:

❏ the skills, leadership, or other personal characteristics of that individual are essential to fulfilling the nonprofit's mission;

❏ few, if any other individuals with these characteristics are available to the nonprofit; and, to a somewhat lesser extent,

❏ any individuals are especially dedicated to the nonprofit's mission, as perhaps evidenced by their willingness to contribute effort, funds or other resources to that mission.

Thus, the departure of a charismatic spokesperson or pharmacist working in a nonprofit rural health clinic could cause great loss. In contrast, any one of several drivers of the nonprofit's vans — someone who could fairly readily be replaced by another equally qualified driver at the same wage — may be less of a key person within the nonprofit.

Valuable Assets at Risk

Any well-managed organization that relies on computers to operate should have virtually instant access to several internal people or outside contractors who know how to operate the system and troubleshoot the computer hardware and software. Yet examples of critical skills residing in a single staff member or volunteer abound in the nonprofit sector, due to perpetual resource challenges.

It is a mistake, however, to think that a nonprofit's most valuable people are always high up on its letterhead or organization chart. The employees or volunteers who have direct daily contact with a nonprofit's regular clients often have the greatest impact — positive or negative — on how effectively a nonprofit actually carries out the mission among the actual people that its charter and its managers only envision. Again, if there is only one person on a nonprofit's staff who knows how to manage the computer program that generates mailings to the nonprofit's regular contributors, that one person may be most valuable to that nonprofit.

The value of the individuals on a nonprofit's board of directors varies with the skills or other qualities each board member brings to the organization. Personal dedication, vision, leadership, public image and, in some cases, direct contributions of funds or other property certainly increase a board member's value. Moreover, even though board members normally leave the daily management of a nonprofit in the hands of its paid staff, some board members do bring special financial, program-design, or mission-specific skills that are essential to a nonprofit's daily activities.

Three additional groups — a nonprofit's clients, its large/influential donors, and the supporting public — provide key value to the organization. The people in these three groups are best thought of as groups, rather than individuals from the strategic risk management standpoint. For example, a nonprofit's client population should:

❑ increase rather than shrink;

❑ be happy that the nonprofit is truly meeting their needs rather than complaining (especially to the media) that the nonprofit is failing them; and

❑ cooperate with the nonprofit's staff, rather than trying to *beat the system*, so that everyone's morale is enhanced.

The group of major donors, except for a dozen or so truly major donors or grant-making foundations with whom the nonprofit's executive director and board chairperson should have some direct personal contact, should:

❑ increase rather than shrink, both in numbers and in the size of their average donation;

❑ come to feel more closely attached to *their* nonprofit, especially so that they encourage others to become major donors;

❑ become potential dedicated volunteers or even new, creative board members to more personally serve the nonprofit.

For strategic risk management purposes, the general public is key to a nonprofit's success to the extent that the public:

❑ is aware of the nonprofit's name and generally sympathetic to its mission, rather than being unaware or opposed; and, as a consequence,

❑ responds generously to the nonprofit's fund-raising efforts, with some members of the public becoming volunteers to, or major supporters of, the nonprofit.

Groups Versus Individuals

We suggest that the key people beyond a nonprofit's officers and staff be considered as groups rather than individuals in a strategic risk management sense, because of the sheer numbers of people within some of the constituencies with which a nonprofit deals. Of course, in phone conversations or in person, wherever feasible, the officers and staff of nonprofits should deal as personally as possible with people as individuals, rather than as members of groups. Personalized treatment — valuing individuals for their own worth — enhances their self-esteem, energy, loyalty and generosity toward the nonprofit — all of which reduce downside threats of accidental loss and build upside opportunities for gain for any nonprofit.

Property

A nonprofit's property can be categorized as:

- real property (land, buildings, and things permanently attached to them),

- equipment (machinery, appliances and vehicles),

- records detailing the organization's daily activities,

- the general furniture and contents in the nonprofit's facilities, and

- intangible property (rights evidenced by such documents such as copyrights and licenses).

Except for items of intangible property, an organization can possess property by either owning or leasing it.

With few exceptions, the items of property that are essential to a nonprofit's mission are — from a strategic risk management perspective — little different from the kinds of property that are crucial to the success of any other organization. In inventorying your nonprofit's property, be watchful for items in each of the categories listed and — for each item — ask, "Is this item vitally important to this nonprofit's mission?" Many items are not really critical. Lots of your furniture, decorations, routine office equipment, or a typical vehicle that has no mission-related special equipment are all examples of nonessential property that pose no special risk management concerns. .

Mission-Critical Question Tree

To determine if an item of property is mission critical: Ask, "Is this item vitally important to this nonprofit's mission?"

If "No" = Not a risk.

If "Yes, this is an essential item."

Then ask: "Do we have, or could we quickly buy or rent, a suitable replacement if anything happened to this particular item?"

If "Yes," you are strategically managing your risk.

If "No, we don't have a ready replacement," then you need to take action to strategically manage your risk.

But if your answer is "Yes, this is an essential item," then go on to ask, "Do we have, or could we quickly buy or rent, a suitable replacement if anything happened to this particular item?" If "Yes," is this replacement process in writing, tested and reviewed periodically? If your answer to this second question is, "No, we don't have a ready replacement," then take action. Arrange somehow for a backup for this key item of property so that your nonprofit can continue serving its clients even if this mission-critical item of property is, for any reason, no longer available.

These mission-related questions can highlight many important property values, but some major property with high value often rests in surprising places. Some such places are filing cabinets, computer disks, and other records-storage media where the data essential for a nonprofit's operations often reside. Records relating to a nonprofit's present and past clients, donors, employees, volunteers and contractors are all sources of information that the nonprofit may need at any time just to keep operating. Other crucial documents are the nonprofit's articles of incorporation, bylaws and tax-exempt determination letters. The real value of these records can go well beyond the expense of recreating or replacing them, if indeed this is possible. Their value — the true loss they potentially pose — is the extra expense the nonprofit will have to incur if it no longer has these records.

For almost any nonprofit, its mission is its most valuable asset — and an intangible one at that. An intangible asset is something of value that cannot be touched or seen. You will not find any of a nonprofit's intangible assets when you walk through its facilities. You may, however, see documentation of its intangible properties, particularly in picture frames on its walls.

Most items of intangible property are legal rights, typically evidenced by *licenses, contracts* or *certificates*. For example, if a nonprofit is a tenant in the offices it occupies, the lease is the contract that documents its right to use those offices for a specified period under certain conditions (including paying rent and not intentionally damaging the property). The *lease* is not the right; it is only evidence of the right. The right to occupy the property — the leasehold — is the intangible property that has value. Similarly, *licenses* to collect funds for community-service purposes, *permits* to hold public parades or conduct informational picketing, as well as postal permits to send mail through the United States Postal Service at reduced rates are evidence of the legal rights or privileges to engage in these activities. It is the rights and privileges that have value, but these rights and privileges are so crucial to many nonprofits that the documentary evidence is prized for what it represents. Many of these rights flow from the federal or state statutes that authorize the creation and chartering of nonprofit organizations to engage in specified types of community-service activities and, while properly doing so, to be excused from paying most taxes. This nonprofit status can be an extraordinarily crucial — yet totally intangible — mission-critical item of property for most nonprofits.

Income

Nonprofits spend money fulfilling community-serving missions. Typically, this income derives from a variety of sources, such as:

❑ donations from individuals and corporations;

❑ grants from government agencies and foundations;

❑ fees for services that the nonprofit provides (paid by clients directly or by third parties);

❑ income from the sale of goods and services unrelated to the nonprofit's community-serving activities; and

❑ investment earnings on the nonprofit's accumulated funds.

Reliable, detailed information on these income sources is more likely to come from a nonprofit's financial statements, than from any survey of its operations or tour of its facilities. Although such a survey or tour may yield some interesting surprises, especially about unanticipated expense leaks that drain away expected net income.

Regardless of their source, income streams are vital to strategic risk management. For downside threats of accidental losses, strategic risk management strives to prevent or minimize events that interfere with revenue streams or create unexpected expenses. The corresponding aim for upside opportunities for gains is to increase revenues and reduce expenses through creative managerial insight.

To help visualize managing both these downside and upside risks, picture a mountain stream flowing through a box that is suspended within the center of the stream. As the stream water flows into the box, a small portion of the water is immediately diverted into a holding tank that sits on the stream's bank and a nutrient is added to the water before it flows out of the box. Hence the water flowing out of the box and back into the stream is changed.

The box represents a nonprofit organization that serves the public and the stream represents the money in the community. The water flowing into the box is the nonprofit's income from various sources. The water that flows through the box represents the funds the nonprofit spends to carry out its public service goal — essentially all the nonprofit's expenses for materials, salaries, rent and other operating costs. The nutrient added to the water as it passes through the box signifies that these funds have served a public purpose or somehow bettered the community, reflecting the nonprofit's mission. The small amount of stream water diverted into the holding tank on the stream's bank portrays the latest addition to the nonprofit's accumulated fund balance, which is represented by the total amount of water in this tank at any given time.

This flow entering the box depicts the nonprofit's normal, unsurprising stream of income and expenses; the volume of nutrients added to the water exiting the box represents the benefit the nonprofit has provided its clients in the community.

Traditional risk management, protecting against downside threats of accidental loss, strives to maintain this normal flow. Thus, traditional risk management:

- ❑ *safeguards the flow of income* into the nonprofit making sure that the anticipated funds from grants, donations, fees, sale of goods and services unrelated to the nonprofit's mission, and investment earnings continue as expected;

- ❑ *continues productive activities*, enabling the nonprofit to add revenue to the stream that benefits the community;

- ❑ *captures and conservatively invests* a small portion of the money that flows through the nonprofit so that its accumulated fund balance remains appropriate for its overall level of activity; and

- ❑ *responsibly directs the flow of money* back into the community to assure that it flows into the intended channels, rather than being wasted on needless expenses or activities unrelated to the nonprofit's exempt purpose.

Strategic risk management also performs these income-safeguarding activities, but it goes further, seeking upside opportunities to enlarge the volume of the income stream and enrich the community-service benefits that the nonprofit releases downstream. Thus, on the upside, strategic risk management seeks insightful ways to:

1. increase to unexpected levels the flow of funds into the nonprofit;

2. add new, higher-quality services into the community from which it can more fully benefit;

3. target more precisely the outflow of funds so that the nonprofit can better serve the community; and

4. increase the operating efficiency of the funds in the accumulated fund balance so that a greater proportion of the nonprofit's aggregate income can be devoted to its community-serving mission.

For these financial assets, *traditional* risk management protects against a great number of threats that may interfere with the flow before it reaches, is within, or goes beyond your nonprofit. *Strategic* risk management extends even further to find and implement opportunities for nourishing these sources of revenue before, inside, and after they reach your nonprofit. These threats and opportunities will be the focus of the next two major sections of this chapter.

Reputation

As Thomas Paine wrote, "Character is much easier kept than recovered." A nonprofit's reputation — its standing in others' eyes and hearts — arguably is the key to all its other values. With an excellent reputation, a nonprofit can readily attract public donations, as well as foundation and government grants; skilled and eager board members, employees and volunteers; and willing, cooperative clients for its community services; buyers for any goods or services it sells; and public officials who regulate its activities. With a poor reputation, a nonprofit is in danger of losing everything. The nonprofit's donor base shrinks, its pool of volunteers diminishes, enthusiasm for board service wanes, opportunities to partner with other nonprofits dwindle, obtaining public-sector funding through grants or contracts often becomes difficult or impossible, and the organization exhausts its resources responding to adverse press.

Strategic risk management recognizes both the downside threats and the upside opportunities that lie at the heart of reputational assets. To control threats to a nonprofit's reputation, strategic risk management calls for avoiding any conduct by any officers or employees that, if it came to public attention, would reflect badly on the nonprofit. Similarly, if incidents that could tarnish the nonprofit's image do occur, the nonprofit's management should make special efforts to reply positively, especially in:

❑ responding to the needs of any individuals who may have been harmed in these incidents; and

❑ taking and, if appropriate, publicizing steps to prevent similar incidents in the future.

To seize upside risks for enhancing a nonprofit's reputation, its managers are watchful for events or for actions by its employees or volunteers that offer opportunities to portray the nonprofit in a highly favorable public light.

Threats—Ways Critical Asset Values Can Surprisingly Plummet

Just trying to think of all the threats that may strike the mission-essential people, property, income and reputation can be very difficult. There are certainly the obvious threats. For example, your offices may burn or experience a flood or earthquake, destroying your furniture, equipment and records. If your nonprofit owns vehicles, they may be involved in roadway or parking lot accidents that can cause property damage and injuries. If sued, your nonprofit surely will incur legal costs, even if these suits are groundless. Or some of your volunteers, donors, grantors or fee-paying clients may find new, more appealing avenues for their generosity. Such changes in loyalties have happened to other nonprofits; soon they may strike yours.

Beyond the obvious threats, startling new ones jump out of the headlines almost daily. Airliners have become guided missiles; could one now be aimed at your nonprofit's building? Suicide bombers seek places crowded with their *godless enemies* in which to sacrifice themselves; could such a bomber be waiting in your lobby? Anthrax bacilli have been crawling out of strangely addressed envelopes and packages; are there any such envelopes or packages in your morning mail? Children have been snatched by enraged adults in revenge for wrongs the kidnappers believe they have suffered at the hands of these children's parents; are any of your nonprofit's clients truly enraged by your organization's supposedly wrongful treatment of them?

Beyond raising troublesome questions, these news events can provide a good foundation for constructive strategic risk management, if only to encourage a nonprofit's managers to broaden their view of what is *normal* and what the nonprofit should be ready to take in stride without shocked surprise. With sound strategic risk management in place, a nonprofit's *normal* expectations change. Normal grows from hopes for *no accidents* and *no unusual bequests with lots of strings attached* to asking, "How many accidents should we expect?" "How bad could they be?" "How should we prepare to deal with the ones we cannot prevent?" and "When we get a strange bequest that is subject to lots of conditions, what is the range of responses we can give that best serves our mission?" Strategic risk management looks ahead to what might happen, prepares for the reasonably likely bad or good possibilities, and says "If that happens, bad or good, we are ready! In that case, here is what we will do."

Identifying threats by drawing on your own experience, by remembering what has happened to people you know, or by staying alert to the news gives only episodic flashes of the causes of loss for a nonprofit. Even a review of the insurance policies that a nonprofit might purchase would generate only a partial summary of the causes of potential accidents, because insurance policies exclude or are totally silent about many possible causes of loss. Furthermore, none of the causes of loss that these random approaches suggest gives any clues about the probability, magnitude, predictability or mission criticality of the accidents they may cause.

A more systematic analysis of threats of accidental losses to a nonprofit breaks the process into three steps. Begin by grouping the *sources* of the threats that can cause these losses. Then look at the *dimensions* of these threats. And finally, review how these *causes* of loss can damage a nonprofit's mission-critical values.

Categories of Accident Threats—Natural, Human and Economic

No list can enumerate all the events or circumstances that may lead to accidental losses — if all the events called *accidents* could be so fully detailed before they happen, these events would not be accidents. However, even though the future is not fully predictable, there are three fundamental categories of causes of loss that do sharpen our analysis of how accidents happen and, consequently, how they can be prevented. The categories are natural, human and economic causes. The accompanying chart shows common examples of cause of loss in each of these three categories.

Causes of Loss: Natural, Human and Economic

Some Natural Perils - Forces of nature; no human intervention

Cave-in	Landslide/mudslide	Rust
Collapse	Lightning	Temperature extremes
Drought	Meteors	Tides
Earthquake	Mildew	Tidal waves
Evaporation	Mold	Uncontrollable vegetation
Erosion	Perils of the air (such as icing	Vermin
Fire of natural origin	and clear-air turbulence)	Volcanic eruption
Flood	Perils of the sea (such as	Water
Hall	icebergs, waves, sandbars, and	Weeds
Humidity extremes	reefs)	Wind (tornado, hurricane, typhoon,
Ice	Rot	and tempest)

Some Human Perils - Actions of one individual or a small group of individuals

Arson	Fire and smoke of human origin	Sonic boom
Chemical leakage	Labor union strikes (direct effects)	Terrorism
Industrial contamination	Molten materials	Theft, forgery, fraud
Discrimination	Pollution (smoke, water, noise)	Toppling of high-piled objects
Electrical overload	Power outage	Vandalism, malicious mischief
Embezzlement	Riot	Vibration
Expropriation (confiscation)	Sabotage	Water hammer
Explosion of human origin	Shrinkage	

Some Economic Perils - Actions of large groups of people who act independently responding to particular conditions - not in concert

Changes in consumer tastes	Inflation	Consequence of strikes
Currency fluctuations	Obsolescence	Technological advances
Depression (recession)	Stock market declines	War

Source: *Essentials of Risk Management*, Third Edition, Volume 1, Insurance Institute of America

Natural Causes of Loss

No one can stop natural causes of loss — earthquakes, floods, blizzards and wildfires ignited by lightning — from occurring, but steps can be taken before and after they happen to reduce their destructive effects. Some control measures are truly long term, such as opting not to locate a nonprofit's facilities on ground that is frequently flooded, or, after suffering several floods, opting to move to higher ground. Other controls are more immediate. For example, when flood warnings are issued, move the particularly crucial contents of a building to its upper floors or to a completely different location. Other controls — such as postflood cleanup — become operative after the natural cause of loss has passed. Nonprofit organizations generally are as vulnerable to natural causes of loss as are other organizations and individuals.

Human Causes of Loss

Through ordinary carelessness, culpable negligence or recklessness, or outright criminal misconduct, humans cause losses that are accidental (having unintended consequences) from the perspective of the persons or organizations that suffer these losses. The resulting accidental loss may fall on the person or organization whose conduct is faulty, as would be the case if the staff of a nonprofit fails to perform adequate maintenance on a vehicle that one morning will not start.

Or one person's wrongful action or inaction may harm other specific individuals or organizations, who may then bring legal claims against the individual doing wrong, as well as any organization on whose behalf or under whose supervision the wrongdoer may have been acting. Wrongful action that causes harm to one or more specific individuals or organizations is a *civil wrong*, either a *breach of contract* (if the wrong grows out of a contractual relationship) or a *tort* (if the wrong does not relate to a contract). Failure to fulfill a promise given in a written or oral contract is the most frequent contractual wrong. *Negligence* (failure to take the legally required degree of care for the safety of another) is a frequent basis for tort claims.

Other wrongful acts that not only harm particular individuals or organizations but also go so far as to endanger the community as a whole are crimes. *Criminal wrongs* are prosecuted by the local, state or federal government on behalf of all the people. An individual or organization found guilty of a crime is subject to fines, imprisonment, loss of many rights and privileges, and often a duty to pay restitution to those directly harmed be the criminal conduct.

A nonprofit may engage in or allow conduct that constitutes both civil and criminal wrongs. This would be conduct for which not only the nonprofit as an organization may be found liable, but its employees or volunteers who were personally involved and the nonprofit's officers who authorized the wrongful conduct may be found personally liable. For example, the CEO's decision to allow members of his *inner circle* to use the nonprofit's credit card for personal expenses, such as groceries and dry cleaning, without requiring reimbursement constitutes embezzlement of the nonprofit's resources. All persons found to have embezzled funds could face criminal prosecution. Or a nonprofit's failure to provide adequate supervision of infants in a nursery could result in charges of criminal child abuse and neglect for the organization, the employees involved in the infant's care and the board, after an infant suffers severe dehydration.

Economic Causes of Loss

Human causes of loss involve individuals or small groups acting independently — careless drivers, thieves, vandals or criminal co-conspirators are examples. In contrast, economic causes of loss arise from the acts of governments or of large numbers of individuals or organizations acting similarly but largely independently. Examples of economic causes of loss are wars, regulatory changes, shifts in technology, changes in consumer preferences, boycotts, and recessions or depressions. For organizations properly prepared to practice true strategic risk management, such economic causes of loss may also be upside opportunities for growth.

Nonprofits are especially sensitive to economic causes of loss. For example, when recessions are feared or occur, a nonprofit's income from donations is likely to diminish, as is its corps of volunteers, many of whom may need to focus on paying employment to bolster their household incomes. Any federal or state tax code change that restricts the tax deductibility of contributions or bequests to nonprofits also will reduce a nonprofit's income. Moreover, if the activities of a nonprofit, or its basic mission, become embroiled in bitter political controversy, any resulting public demonstrations or consumer boycotts are likely to both reduce the nonprofit's income and disrupt its normal activities.

Characteristics of Accident Threats

Recognizing that natural, human and economic causes of loss threaten the value of mission-critical people, property, income and reputation provides a good basic framework for gauging the threats of accidental losses that a nonprofit must manage. However, knowing that such losses are possible is *not* enough. To use strategic risk management resources most effectively, a nonprofit's managers need to consider three characteristics of the potential losses from these threats:

1. Frequency of losses — How often will they happen?

2. Magnitude of losses — How bad will they be? How much will they cost?

3. Predictability of losses — How sure are we?

In general, a nonprofit should give greater strategic risk management attention to those threats of accidental loss where:

❑ losses are more likely, rather than less likely;

❑ losses are larger, rather than smaller; and

❑ losses are less predictable, rather than more predictable.

For example, all three of these guidelines probably would lead the managers of a nonprofit located on the Gulf of Mexico to pay more strategic risk management attention to the threat of hurricane damage to its headquarters building than to the threat that one of its vans may be stolen. At any given location on the Gulf Coast, hurricanes probably are more likely, more severe, and less predictable than are van thefts.

The logic of these three guidelines may not always be clear, and at times they may lead to conflicting priorities. The reasoning behind the first two guidelines — putting high priority on threats of the more frequent and larger losses should be evident. Preventing these losses or reducing their cost saves a nonprofit more money, thus preserving more resources to devote to its community-service mission. The purpose of the third guideline — giving greater priority to the less predictable threat — is to reduce uncertainty, build confidence and reduce worry among a nonprofit's management and clients. When losses are predictable then — regardless of how frequent or severe these losses may be — they become more manageable — more easily taken in stride as regular business expenses rather than accidental losses.

For example, the managers of a special residential school for developmentally disabled children know that, in more years than not, some students' relatives or friends who visit the school during the Fall Student Talent Show Gala and fundraiser are going to damage or steal some school equipment or supplies. One year visitors accidentally started a fire while warming hors d'hoevres in the school's kitchen. That the school will suffer some damage at each gala is quite certain; how much damage can be quite unpredictable and a source of worry for some of the school's board members. These members put high priority on hiring outside security guards to supervise all events during the gala to make sure nothing dangerous happens and on purchasing a special event liability insurance policy just in case someone, perhaps even a group, gets badly hurt during these festivities and sues the school. At first, some board members thought the gala posed no great risks, but at a special meeting, the more worried board members convinced the others that the unpredictability of the magnitude of the school's possible accidental losses during the gala merited special strategic risk management attention.

Because these three guidelines for prioritizing risk take account of subjective factors, require insights that no one person may possess, and call for some collective judgments, it is good strategic risk management practice to involve a committee in setting risk management priorities. The work of such a committee is discussed in Chapter 3.

Effects of Accidents on Mission-Critical Values

For every organization, the full range of natural, human and economic causes of loss can threaten the value of its key people, property, income and reputation assets. Any cause of loss potentially can strike the value of any asset. However nonprofits, probably more than profit-seeking organizations, are particularly vulnerable to unanticipated events that impair their key assets all at once. Unlike other organizations that have separate product lines, geographical divisions or client bases, a nonprofit's mission often tightly intertwines all of its key assets. For many a nonprofit, a single severe accident can bring down the entire house.

To get the picture, consider again the annual gala at the special residential school. Suppose, hypothetically, that the parents of one of the resident students are estranged and — unknown to the school administration — are having a bitter custody battle over their one child. These quarrelling parents normally do not see or talk to each other except through their lawyers or counselors in family court, but, on this occasion, both parents come separately to see their son perform in the talent portion of the gala. One of the parents becomes enraged and, in an effort to seize possession of their child, pulls out a gun and shoots the other parent and a teacher who was trying to separate the quarreling couple. (Similar events could occur at large public events sponsored by any nonprofit that serves vulnerable clients — again, all without the management of the sponsoring nonprofit being aware of the danger waiting to explode from within some members of the crowd.) The shootings appear on the local, but not the national, network news.

The school's losses to its mission-critical assets quite likely include:

- loss of people, as parents withdraw their children from the school, staff members leave for safer employment, and individual donors and foundation grantors shift their loyalties and funds to other schools where children are more safely nurtured.

- loss of property, actually the use of property, during the week the police cordon off portions of the school's campus, to investigate.

- loss of income, when tuition and grants drop precipitously in the wake of adverse publicity about the school.

- loss of reputation, when the general public and even the administrators of other educational facilities that had been referring students to this special school wonder how the administration of this school could have failed to be aware of the hostility between the parents fighting for custody of their child.

Meanwhile, the top administrators of this special school might well be left wondering what they would have done if they had known the estranged parents were feuding so violently. Would the school have barred one or both parents from the gala? Would the school have assigned separate security staff to each parent? Did the school have a clear duty to do anything? Because the school administration had not considered any of these questions before holding the gala, this special school's whole existence was at risk of collapse.

Opportunities—Ways Critical Values Can Surprisingly Skyrocket

The remaining pages of this chapter turn upside down everything its previous pages have said. But do not stop reading. This dichotomy can be of real benefit to your mission. Risk — *a measure of the possibility that the future may be surprisingly different from what we expect* — has two opposite sides. We have seen that threats may make the future surprisingly *bad*; now we look at how opportunities may make the future surprisingly *good*.

Your approach to examining this good side of risk is much like your approach to the bad side. We are still going to be focused on a nonprofit's key assets — its people, property, income and reputation — only here you look for opportunities to nourish these assets, not threats that may destroy them. And we are still looking for surprising things — not routine, planned, traditional ways of gradually enhancing a nonprofit's resources. Planned growth certainly is important to nonprofits, and many managers in the nonprofit sector are highly skilled at enhancing an organization's overall operations and the lives of those whom these nonprofits serve. But these tried techniques of *traditional* nonprofit risk management are not *strategic* risk management, especially not strategic risk management for the *surprising upside opportunities*.

Sources of Opportunities

We noted in Chapter 1 that, just as cause of loss produces accidental losses, so managerial insights generate opportunities for gain. There are two broad sources of managerial insights — innovations and adaptations. *Innovation* is a change in technology, operating procedures, products, marketing, or any other aspect of a nonprofit's activities, that its management actually creates — a new way of doing something that is better than anyone has ever done it previously. *Adaptation* is readiness to adjust to change that already is occurring or has occurred. Innovation requires creativity; adaptability requires preparedness; *managerial insight* is the essential source of both creativity and preparedness.

As one example, a nonprofit's leadership innovates when it broadens its mission to embrace a significant new group of clients and moves its headquarters to a location that is more central for this wider group. In contrast, its leadership adapts when it finds that its traditional client base has moved to another area and the nonprofit moves its headquarters to follow its clients. (In still further contrast, the management of this nonprofit could have neither innovated nor have been prepared to adapt — it could have tried to serve its traditional clients from its old headquarters. And, without innovation or preparedness to adapt, this nonprofit could very easily have failed for lack of managerial insight. But, having the insight and the initiative to redefine its client base and to move its headquarters, this nonprofit seized the opportunity.)

Characteristics of Opportunities

Both threats and opportunities have three very crucial characteristics: probability, magnitude and predictability. In deciding whether to pursue an opportunity, a nonprofit's managers need to consider whether:

❑ their insight, the source of their opportunity for growth, has a great or a small chance of succeeding,

❑ the success will be great or small, and

❑ they have good reason to be highly confident of success or worried that their innovation or attempt to adapt may fail.

As an illustration, suppose the executive director of a nonprofit that provides service animals to mobility-challenged people recognizes that bobble-head dolls of professional sports stars are very popular and decides to adapt them as a fund-raising idea for his nonprofit. He suggests to his board that this nonprofit should contract with the manufacturer of these dolls to design and make plastic dog dolls bearing the nonprofit's logo to sell to raise funds. In reviewing this proposal, the board needs to think about both the potential negatives of the campaign, as well as ways its effectiveness could be enhanced. Some issues of enhancement might be:

❑ the total potential revenue that might be earned from selling the dolls given the population of persons likely to make a purchase in order to support the nonprofit,

❑ the potential publicity the nonprofit might garner by undertaking an unusual promotion such as this one, and

❑ whether there is a possibility to enhance the revenue-generating opportunity by partnering with a manufacturer that would donate the dolls to the nonprofit.

Effects of Opportunities on Mission-Critical Values

Insightful ways to grow a nonprofit's key people, property, income and reputation assets abound, but they are difficult to enumerate in the abstract. Insights spring from specific situations that creative minds have time to ponder. Nonetheless, it is possible to provide you with some examples that you may wish to adapt to your nonprofit — examples that may inspire you to innovate in totally creative ways.

■ **People** — To increase the cost-effectiveness of their volunteer recruitment efforts, the branch offices of several youth-mentoring programs launch a coordinated volunteer recruitment drive aimed at attracting male mentors into their programs. By combining resources, the three groups are in position to afford radio spots that feature a local sports star touting the benefits a mentor derives from participating in a youth-mentoring program.

These three nonprofits also agree to exchange their newsletter mailing lists so that the volunteers and donors of each group learn from what the others are doing. Each of these cooperating groups asks their volunteers to read these newsletters (or anything else) for ideas about what their local branch should do differently to be more effective. A side benefit to this decision could be each participating volunteer will feel more important to the nonprofit, increasing volunteers' commitment and reducing dropout rates.

■ **Property** — When a nonprofit preschool was bequeathed a very old dilapidated mansion located nearly a mile from the main campus of the school, its board at first thought the property was essentially worthless, not fit for educational uses and too costly to renovate to meet state standards. But one board member was inspired to look into the old building's history and discovered that it had once belonged to a renowned pioneer in the original settling of the region. Armed with this insight, the board can move on to consider how best to restore and make use of this mansion — perhaps as an historic bed-and-breakfast (a surprising source of income for the school), or perhaps as a renovated facility that a local hotel chain would like to buy as a commercial property, adding significantly to the capital accumulated in the school's endowment fund.

> Intelligent and continuing communication with key stakeholders is arguably the primary risk response. Communication *conditions* stakeholders for the unexpected and the degree to which an organization has prepared for them.
>
> — H. Felix Kloman Editor, *Risk Management Reports*

■ **Income** — To increase large gifts from individuals, an inner-city family recreation program holds a press conference to announce one substantial donation it has just received (donor anonymous, of course) and specifically what it plans to do with the money — something that has great public emotional appeal. The nonprofit's spokesperson goes further to explain what this nonprofit would do — something different, but equally appealing — if it received additional substantial donations.

A group of six youth-serving nonprofits in a large metropolitan area band together to form a purchasing cooperative for the purpose of obtaining better rates on various contracts for goods and services. None of the six nonprofits has a full-time finance director or other person who can coordinate purchases and review contracts for the purchase of goods and services. The cooperative is able to afford the services of a part-time independent contractor who obtains bids for the six groups. The strategy increases the buying power of each nonprofit while reducing the staff time required to arrange significant purchases.

■ **Reputation** — A nonprofit camp learns about a scandal facing a camp in a neighboring county. A long-time staff member of the camp was arrested for trafficking in child pornography, and was found to have used the computer provided by the camp to download and send pornographic images. The staff member had no prior arrests, and the camp's screening process did not raise any red flags. The employee was punctual, responsive, and well liked by staff and campers. The camp decides to develop a media communications strategy so that it is prepared to face the media should the organization come under scrutiny as fallout from the neighboring camp's crisis or face a scandal in the future. The camp obtains pro bono assistance from a public relations firm and crafts a series of statements about its operations. The CEO of the camp attends an interactive class on the topic of on-camera interviews.

Downside and Upside Risks

Differences —

Sources:	Threats versus insights
Results:	Losses versus gains
Techniques for managing them:	Risk control and risk financing versus innovation and adaption

Similiarities —

Cause:	Uncertainty
Measured by:	Probability, Magnitude and Predictability

Both require strategic risk management attention

Strategic risk management focuses on both downside risks *and* upside risks. Traditional risk management focuses only on downside risks.

Summary

This chapter has dealt with the second step of the general strategic risk management process: appraise both downside and upside risks. To put this step into the vernacular, a nonprofit's managers are wise to put their money where their mouth is by providing the biggest bang for the buck. This is done by determining which assets (people, property, income and reputation) have more value to the ongoing fulfillment of the nonprofit's mission. Once this is determined, the managers can focus their resources on the support of these life-or-death assets for the organization.

CHAPTER 3

Putting the Pieces Together
The Strategic Risk Management
Process in Action

T his chapter explains the five steps in the strategic risk
management process, illustrating how it works in both
countering threats of loss and positioning your nonprofit to
take advantage of opportunities for gain.

As we discussed in Chapter 1, strategic risk management is built
around a five-step decision process. This process is similar to the
decision process that *traditional* risk management employs in dealing
with only the downside risks of accidental losses, but the concepts
and terminology of *strategic* risk management are broader and more
inclusive than those of traditional risk management. These five steps
are:

1. **Establish the Context**

    ❏ Determine the Organization's Risk Management Profile

    ❏ Set Risk Management Goals

2. **Appraise Risks**

    ❏ Identify Risks

    ❏ Prioritize Risks

3. **Decide What to Do and Communicate Your Decision**

4. **Act on Your Decision**

5. **Follow up and Adjust**

Step 1 — Establish the Context

Just as a gardener who ignores the importance of proper soil preparation and plants acid-sensitive plants in highly acidic soil risks sickly results, failure to thoughtfully consider the context for an organization's risk management program could lead to disappointment down the road. Instead of a multifaceted program that reduces injuries at the nonprofit's recreation facility and enables it to expand its menu of services, the risk management program may be doomed to fail even before the first loss-prevention or risk-financing technique is put to the test. To increase the odds of success and establish a suitable foundation for the activities to follow, a nonprofit should begin by looking at its history, culture and operations. The questions that follow will help you get started. (Some of these questions are for organizations that have started doing risk management, perhaps a few years ago; others are for organizations that have never had a risk management program.)

❑ What has been the history of risk management in this nonprofit? What lessons has the organization learned from past attempts?

❑ What is the risk-taking culture of this nonprofit? Does the organization tend to shy away from risks and pursue the most conservative course of action? Or does the organization take risks carelessly without giving adequate consideration to losses that might stem from risk taking?

❑ What is the general attitude of the members of the board of directors? Do they readily support the development of a risk management program, especially one that considers both downside and upside risks? Are they driving the creation of a program or simply following the staff's lead? Are they willing to be involved in policy-level activities related to risk management? Or have they expressed a desire to place full responsibility for the program on the shoulders of the staff? Do they take active responsibility for knowing the major risks and how the organization is responding to them?

❑ How is the staff likely to react to the announcement that the nonprofit will be undertaking a risk management program? Will there be volunteers amongst the staff eager to serve on a risk management committee?

❑ What is the culture of the organization with respect to safety and risk management? Does it already have a track record of identifying and addressing dangers or will this be the first effort?

❑ What breadth of effort is likely to enjoy most success at this time? For example, is starting with one operational area a good approach to easing into the discipline of risk management, or would it make more sense to start with a comprehensive, organization-wide program that systematically engages all areas or departments within the nonprofit?

❑ Is a single person assigned both responsibility and authority for the risk management program?

Answering the previous questions will allow you to create a profile of the organization that will be invaluable as you proceed with the remaining steps in the process. For example, if you are likely to face resistance from members of a staff that perceives the organization as policy-heavy, you need to focus on practical risk management strategies that do not require voluminous documentation. In another instance, if the board feels that risk management is simply an administrative task, you need to include an examination of governance risks in the program.

Step 2 — Appraise Risks

In this second step, a nonprofit sets about identifying its portfolio of risks and continues by assigning values or weights to the risks. Remember that in Chapter 1 we defined risk as *a measure of the possibility that the future may be surprisingly different from what we expect.*

Who's on First?

One of the first decisions your nonprofit must make before beginning to appraise risks is "Who should be involved?" In many instances it make sense to charge the same group of people with undertaking the five steps in the process, rather than use one group for risk appraisal and a second group for strategy identification. It is important to include individuals who have operations-level familiarity with your nonprofit, as well as persons from different rungs on your organizational ladder. Do not make the mistake of naming only senior managers to the risk management committee. Doing so will make it more difficult to get support from staff and volunteers at all levels down the road.

Risk Appraisal: List Making

In many respects, risk appraisal is a hybrid of list making and brainstorming. The group sets about identifying risks, offering commentary only to clarify and narrowly define the risk. Weighing in with respect to a risk's probability or potential magnitude and looking for both downside risks of potential loss and upside risks of potential gain comes later.

To get an idea how this works, consider the risks facing a nonprofit that sponsors an annual 10K race to raise money for its campaign to promote early testing for prostate cancer. The turnout for the race for the past five years has averaged 200-300 runners. The best turnout was two years ago, when weather conditions on the day of the run were perfect. About 80 percent of the participants pre-register using the form on the nonprofit's Web site. The remaining runners show up the morning of the race and complete a short enrollment form at the onsite registration desks. Some of the risks facing the organization that are related specifically to this event include:

❑ the possibility of bad weather bringing unusually poor attendance, resulting in an overall net financial loss (100 registrants at $25 each are needed to cover the operating expenses of the event, which include advertising, security, T-shirts, bottled water, permit and prizes).

❑ the possibility of greater than expected attendance in the range of 400-500 people.

❑ the possibility that a runner could suffer a serious or fatal injury while participating in the race.

❑ the possibility that an Olympic track medallist who lives nearby announces she is participating and bringing the media and lots of spectators with her.

A group of creative individuals who have lived through the organization's road races will be able to come up with a long list that includes both probable and remote risks.

List Management

In the previous example, we took a snapshot of the risks associated with a single activity. Few nonprofits will be content to limit risk management programs to a single activity or area of operations. So the challenge is coming up with a workable framework that allows the risk management committee to cover the bases. There are various approaches for doing this. Some organizations separate their key programs and services, and appraise risk by program. Others begin with the organization chart and appraise risks by department — sometimes involving subcommittees tasked with identifying the risks in their area. Another approach is to group risks by client segments: risks related to youth programs, risks related to programs serving seniors, and risks related to family activities. In a school serving grades K-8, risks for children in kindergarten through 4th grade may differ somewhat from the risks for children in 5th through 8th grades. There is no single approach that works for every organization. The culture, history, politics and environment of a nonprofit come into play in determining how to go about the task of risk appraisal.

Risk Appraisal: Weights and Measures

The long lists developed in the first stage of risk appraisal can be daunting to even an experienced risk management committee member. A thoughtful, creative group of staff and volunteers can quickly come up with dozens of risks worthy of further review. And it is likely that some of the risks will be so grave that they cause serious concern. It would not be surprising, therefore, to see members of a risk management committee throw their hands up in frustration after spending hours on risk identification. The feeling that "We'll never be able to tackle all of these items" may be expressed. So it is important to move quickly on to measuring and evaluating the identified risks. Doing so will provide a roadmap for risk control and loss prevention activities, as well as the opportunities for gain to follow. It will also reveal that some of the risks initially listed are too remote to worry about for the time being.

Prioritizing risks can take any number of forms. For some risk management committees, the most logical approach is simply to review the various lists and strive to reach consensus about the order of importance. Other groups that prefer to use mathematical tools may choose to assign *frequency* (how often) and *magnitude* (how costly/how beneficial) ratings in order to score the risks. *Frequency* is a *measure of how often the risk is likely to materialize*, or the *probability* of the risk materializing. *Magnitude measures the cost or benefit (in positive or negative terms) should the risk materialize.* On the negative side, magnitude measures "How bad would it be if this happened?" or "How much would it cost?" On the positive side, it measures "How beneficial would it be to the organization?" or "How much do we stand to gain?"

Some organizations base the scores on detailed loss runs or other statistical reports. If these financial documents are not available, assignment of scores may involve a brainstorming discussion where individuals express their views and the facilitator guides the group to consensus. The examples that follow use a scale of 1-10 for frequency and magnitude ratings: 1 = very low frequency or very low magnitude; 4-6 = moderate frequency or moderate magnitude; and 8-10 = high frequency or high magnitude. As you read about the application of this scoring system to a set of risks, keep in mind:

❑ The scoring scale is simply a tool that will enable the ordinal ranking of risks — a starting point for choosing amongst various risks to address through risk management strategies.

❑ Any scoring system that helps you differentiate between catastrophic and ordinary risks will work, such as A-F, 1-100, or High-Medium-Low.

Key Concepts

Frequency = how *often* is the risk likely to materialize?

Magnitude = what *cost* or what *benefit* can we expect if the risk materializes?

❑ Organizations that are new to risk management and feel overwhelmed by the use of a scoring system should consider using a scale with fewer choices, such as High-Medium-Low.

❑ There is no correct score for a particular risk, only a highly subjective score that reflects the opinions of a group of people at a particular point in time.

❑ Experience — yours and others — enriches the process. Keep in mind that the more you know about what has happened to your nonprofit in the past and to other similarly situated nonprofits (with respect to locale, menu of services, volunteer/paid staff mix), the better position you will be in to estimate the probability and magnitude of future events.

To test this process, apply the scoring method to the identified risks of the example 10K run, and consider the scores that might be assigned.

Poor attendance

❑ The possibility of unusually poor attendance, resulting in an overall net financial loss (100 registrants at $25 each are needed to cover the operating expenses of the event, which include advertising, security, T-shirts, bottled water, permit and prizes).

The risk management team might feel that attendance falling below the minimum required for financial viability is exceedingly remote, given that pre-registrations are out-pacing last year's total number. The team might assign a frequency score of "1" indicating a remote risk. On the topic of magnitude, the committee might agree that although a financial loss on the race would be troublesome, the organization could still generate positive publicity from moving forward with the race despite a low turnout. And it could use the low turnout as the basis for a special fundraising appeal to past donors and runners with which to meet the dollar goal of the run. With this in mind, the team might assign a score of "4", indicating low-moderate magnitude. Adding the scores together yields a score of 5 for this risk.

Record Attendance

❑ The possibility of greater-than-expected attendance in the range of 400-500 people.

Risk? But this is a fundraiser's dream come true. On one day a small nonprofit could achieve its fund-raising goal for an entire year. Given the five-year history of the run, the risk management committee may be inclined to assign a relatively low frequency of 2. On a magnitude scale, a rating of 10 might be warranted: twice the expected attendance could be a real boon for the nonprofit. The resulting score of 12 might move this risk into the category that warrants immediate attention. In this case, it is because the risk presents the potential for gain to the organization. Strategic risk management strategies applied to the risk will seek to address the risk of loss or harm, while increasing the probability the nonprofit will reap the positive outcomes.

Unhealthy Outcome

❑ The possibility that a runner could suffer a serious or fatal injury while participating in the race.

When the risk management committee considers this risk, the members will probably discuss the typical fitness of runners in past races, whether there have been any injuries or near misses in the past, and what precautions are already in place that affect frequency or magnitude. For example, the nonprofit may have a policy in place requiring the postponement of the race if the temperature reaches 90 degrees before 9 a.m. This practice reduces the probability of heat-related injuries. Yet registrants are largely unknown to the race organizers and could have any number of unknown or latent health conditions, which would make the race dangerous. This heightens the possibility of harm occurring. After considering these factors, the committee may assign a frequency rating of 2.

With respect to magnitude, the committee is likely to agree initially that a serious injury could be disastrous to the organization. Yet, when it conducts some research on special events sponsored by nonprofits, it may learn that injuries at athletic events are not uncommon, and even the most serious harm — the death of a participant — may not mean the end of the event or the nonprofit. Given the organization's focus on the health and safety of the participants — screening participants by asking health questions on the application form, cautioning participants about the conditioning required to run a 10K, and requiring that first-aid-certified volunteers be stationed at equidistant points — the committee may feel that a critical injury or death would be serious, but not catastrophic, from a financial or public relations perspective. With this in mind, the committee might assign a magnitude rating of 7.

The Media Event

❑ The possibility that an Olympic track medallist who lives nearby will elect to participate, attracting media attention and spectators to the event.

Like the upside risk of better-than-expected attendance, the chance that a celebrity might join the race could yield enormous returns to the nonprofit. The committee may assign a score of 5 to this risk, speculating that the possibility of the champion showing up to support the cause and the community is 50:50. The corresponding magnitude score would also be high — the champion's mere presence at the race could generate the publicity needed to boost the nonprofit's annual fund drive. The champion might also consent to being featured in a short video the nonprofit is developing for use in an endowment campaign. With these benefits in mind, the committee might assign a score of 8 in the magnitude column, bringing the total score for this risk to 13.

When the committee tabulates the scores for the risks associated with the 10K run, the following results are revealed:

	Frequency	Magnitude	Total
Low turnout jeopardizes fundraising goal	1	4	5
Record turnout boosts fund-raising outcomes	2	10	12
Participant dies on route to the finish line	2	7	9
Olympic medallist graces the winner's circle	5	8	13

In a resource-plentiful world (Nirvana for a nonprofit organization), the risk management committee might turn its attention to all of the risks discussed in the 10K example. But we know that the "real world" where nonprofits reside is one filled with perpetually resource-constrained organizations. There are never enough dollars or people to do everything the nonprofit wants and rarely enough resources to cover truly mission-critical activities. As a result, difficult choices must be made.

The rating system proposed in the preceding pages should support this decision-making process by making it easier to see where the organization can get the greatest bang for its buck. Assuming the nonprofit sponsoring the 10K run only has the resources (people, time and money) to address two of the risks, then the risks of greater-than-hoped-for attendance and the possibility of the Olympic medallist participating are those deserving further attention. That further attention consists simply of selecting and applying strategic risk management techniques to either reduce the probability of harm or loss, or increase the possibility of positive net gains.

Step 3 — Decide What to Do and Communicate Your Decision

Many nonprofits report that assigning frequency and magnitude ratings and coming up with an ordinal ranking of risks is the most time-consuming and difficult stage of the process. The good news is that the next step — brainstorming practical strategies — often flows quite freely.

The Risk Management Techniques Menu

Most nonprofits employ a variety of risk management techniques — often without knowing that the discipline of risk management acts as a structural support for the nonprofit's foundation. The techniques may be regarded as sound risk management by some, and as simple common sense, good business practices or even necessary evils by others.

Many complex risk management challenges, such as the desire to protect the young children attending a nonprofit's recreation programs from predators, require a combination of techniques applied thoughtfully to the situation at hand. It is a rare instance when a risk such as the possibility that a young client will suffer harm can be fully addressed with one simple measure. The exception of course, is avoidance, such as when a nonprofit daycare center decides to fill in its in-ground swimming pool to eliminate altogether the risk that a toddler will drown while enrolled in the center's summer program. This choice has implications beyond the safety issue. Filling in the pool may eliminate a potential source of income for the center, as well as a source of pleasure for service recipients.

The following risk management techniques or controls are often found in the nonprofit sector, including organizations that do not know they are practicing good risk management.

1. **Provide Training** — The importance of training is widely appreciated in the nonprofit sector. Nonprofit managers generally recognize that before sending an army of volunteers to a construction site where a community-serving agency is building a home, or in teams to deliver hot meals to elderly residents, an organization should provide instruction concerning:

   ❏ The clients it serves — What the agency should communicate about its clientele to enable the staff to do their jobs.

   ❏ The rules concerning the manner in which services are to be delivered. For example, an agency assisting elderly residents with errands and bill paying may forbid volunteers from loaning their clients money. Or an organization that matches adult mentors with economically disadvantaged children on a one-to-one basis may prohibit overnight outings involving the pair until after they have been closely observed by the organization for six months.

❑ The organization's emergency procedures — What the nonprofit expects and requires its paid staff and volunteers to do in the event they face a crisis while serving the organization.

2. **Provide Safety Equipment and Tools** — Various safety devices are available to paid and volunteer staff working in nonprofit organizations. These range from rubber gloves and face masks in a clinic, to ear plugs used when operating power tools in a community-beautification program, or a warning siren mounted on a fork lift used to move pallets of canned goods and other donated items within the nonprofit's warehouse.

A growing number of nonprofits recognize the inherent risks when a representative sets off in a passenger van or personal automobile to transport clients or materials on the nonprofit's behalf.

3. **Establish Limits, Rules and Requirements** — A nonprofit cannot operate safely without limits, rules and requirements that apply to the nonprofit's staff, as well as people who receive its services or simply visit its premises. The challenge to a nonprofit is to adopt a sufficient number of rules and requirements to adequately protect the assets of the organization, without creating such a tangled web that violation becomes a forgone conclusion. Rules that are ignored are a serious potential liability to the nonprofit. Examples of rules and requirements that are important strategic risk management techniques include:

❑ technology-use rules for the nonprofit's staff, such as prohibiting use of the nonprofit's equipment to transmit messages that are profane or inflammatory;

❑ a client code of conduct requiring that clients show the staff and one another mutual respect;

❑ rules concerning visitors to the nonprofit's premises, such as all visitors must enter through the main entrance and be screened by security personnel;

❑ curfew rules at a residential facility for adults undergoing drug and alcohol rehabilitation;

❑ a prohibition on staff engaging in sexual relationships with clients at a group home; and

❑ the requirement that staff travel in pairs when conducting home visits to families involved in custody disputes.

4. **Screen Staff, Volunteers and Participants** — Matching the most-qualified applicant for a paid or volunteer position with a key post in a nonprofit is no simple task. The Center's publication, *Staff Screening Tool Kit: Building a Strong Foundation Through Careful Staffing*, explores the role of screening in a risk management program, including legal considerations and the various tools available to nonprofits today. One of the important themes of the book is that a one-size fits all approach to screening is generally flawed and frequently inadvisable. During the past decade there has been a great deal of attention paid to the use of criminal history background checks in nonprofits. Yet despite widespread belief to the contrary, the use of these background checks is not advisable in all instances. In many cases these background checks become the focal point of a screening process that ignores potentially valuable tools, such as credential verification and reference checking. The starting point for designing a screening process is an identification of the risks posed by the position. High-risk positions should be subject to more intense scrutiny than low-risk positions. A high-risk position is one in which the staff member or volunteer will have unsupervised contact with vulnerable clients. Or a high-risk position might be one where the candidate will have access to the nonprofit's financial assets. It is a very rare case where every position in an organization warrants a similar screening process. Many nonprofits have personnel in low-, moderate- and high-risk positions.

Appropriate screening can also increase upside risks. Screening should never be simply about identifying bad apples. The key to effective screening is effective matchmaking. A nonprofit that exercises care in the selection of its personnel may find that incoming staff quickly become devoted employees whose contributions continue over several decades. With respect to volunteer screening, a volunteer who is matched with an appropriate assignment may not only feel rewarded and enriched by her experience with the nonprofit, she may decide to make a sizeable financial contribution and persuade others to do so as well.

5. **Supervise** — The importance of supervision cannot be overstated. It is a grave mistake to believe that individuals who have sailed through the nonprofit's screening process and completed the volunteer orientation require little supervision. Supervision is a safety tool that needs to be employed with care and consistency. When an employee or volunteer violates the organization's trust or disregards an important rule or requirement, disciplinary action — up to and including termination in egregious cases — should be applied.

6. **Make Program Design Changes** — One too-often neglected risk management strategy is to make changes in the design of a program to heighten its safety. For example, an organization holding

an annual street fair that attracts 50,000 visitors must recruit and deploy nearly 500 volunteers, including more than 400 spontaneous volunteers. A spontaneous volunteer is typically someone who shows up to assist the day of the event. Due to the nature of the event — a one-day street fair — it makes little sense to devote months to interviews, background checks and reference checks. So the nonprofit sponsor collapses the screening process into a three-question application card that persons wanting to volunteer fill out when they arrive on site the morning of the fair. Given these circumstances, the nonprofit must be creative in identifying suitable jobs for these volunteers that it knows little or nothing about. Rather than assigning a single volunteer to the ticket booth, where he might be handling hundreds of dollars every few minutes, a team of volunteers is assigned to ticket duty, the teams are rotated throughout the day and closely supervised by an employee. Bonded staff members stop by the booths at intervals to retrieve the ticket revenue, and comparisons are made of the sales rates at side-by-side booths. Any time there is less than a desirable amount of time for screening and training, a nonprofit can and should compensate by looking carefully at position and program design.

Sometimes a few simple changes can significantly alter the exposure. One youth-serving program faced a crisis when a member of the organization was sexually molested by a volunteer leader. The member had informed his parents that he was attending a function sponsored by the nonprofit when in fact he was visiting the adult volunteer's home. The organization subsequently decided to publish a schedule of its events and distribute the schedule on a regular basis to parents of members. This simple change in program design and delivery could prevent a similar incident from happening in the future by engaging the parents as partners in protecting their children.

7. Schedule Regular Equipment Maintenance and Repair

— It is wise to set up a routine for safety checks, maintenance and repair. Depending on the nature of your clients and services, there are building codes and licensing requirements to be met. You will want to make certain that you identify all of the federal, state and local regulations and laws that apply to your nonprofit. You will also need a mechanism in place for being updated when these change. You want the mechanism to be the easiest and most reliable for you. Not knowing is not a defense. With respect to maintenance and repair records, routines will help avert injuries and accidents, but if you are sued, you will want to be able to provide proof that you actually fulfilled your *duty of care*. This is where a log (or checklists and repair follow-up sheets) is invaluable. Think of the log as a diary or history of the piece of equipment. Record the date of purchase, manufacturer and serial number. Record who services the equipment

Risk Management Techniques Menu

1. Provide training.
2. Provide safety equipment and tools.
3. Establish limits, rules and requirements.
4. Screen staff, volunteers and participants.
5. Supervise.
6. Make program design changes.
7. Schedule regular equipment maintenance and repair.
8. Develop a crisis management plan and test it.
9. Make your expectations clear and provide explicit direction.
10. Get help from outside experts.
11. Inventory assets.
12. Comply with applicable local, state and federal regulations.
13. Implement workable internal controls.
14. Prepare to pay for some accidental losses.
15. Communicate regularly with stakeholders.

(boiler, fire extinguisher, alarm system, air conditioning condenser), the date of service, advice given, what was maintained, repaired or replaced. A central heating system record might say, fall service; filter replaced.

8. **Develop a Crisis Management Plan and Test It** — Among the downside and upside risks that you have identified are several that would throw the organization into a crisis mode. Fire, natural disasters, workplace violence, a bomb threat, terrorism, utility failure/leak, sudden death and a hostage situation are some examples. As you can see from the list, these are anxiety- and adrenaline-producing scenarios. Crisis management planning develops procedures for leadership roles, evacuation, constituent communication, media relations, cooperative service delivery, and temporary space before the fact, while heads are cooler. If one of these highly out-of-the-ordinary events occurs, the plan provides the basics — who is in charge, who to call and when, where people should gather, what to say to the media — in outline or checklist form. Some organizations find a crisis management committee or team (the building engineer, insurance professional, police and fire officials, and department heads) can focus best on developing and upgrading the plan. While some responses to crisis cannot be rehearsed, others can be simulated, practiced or simply discussed to enhance readiness for the real thing and identify any flaws. After each drill, key personnel should prepare a brief written analysis. Include the name of the organization, the nature of the drill, the address of the site, date and time, participants, observations and follow-up status. Such due diligence helps preserve reputation, and is backup to any insurance claims. In between full-blown drills, tabletop exercises keep the strategies and process fresh in the minds of all staff and clients. For information about creating a crisis management manual, as well as sample forms and record sheets, see the Nonprofit Risk Management Center's book, *Vital Signs: Anticipating, Preventing and Surviving a Crisis in a Nonprofit.*

9. **Make Your Expectations Clear and Provide Explicit Direction** — The people you rely on generally want to succeed. They need clear direction to do so. After all, how clean is clean? There are many standards from wiped down to sterilized. Think of your audience. Put information in terms they will easily understand. You may have to translate instructions into another language, which could be Russian or simplification of technical jargon into everyday terms. You may have to speak more slowly or demonstrate what you want done. One way to test if your direction is being understood is to ask the person to tell you or show you what they think you are asking them to do. Another is to watch for a glazing over of the eyes. Set realistic deadlines. If you mean by 3 p.m. today or by next Tuesday at 5 p.m., do not say ASAP. It will only lead to

disappointment for both parties. With new, complicated or lengthy tasks, it helps to set intermediate deadlines (sometimes called checkpoints) to monitor how the person is proceeding, provide an opportunity for questions and clarification, and correct or reassess what is being done and how. If the person has to work within a budget, provide a dollar range, or give permission to spend up to a set amount without further consultation. Make yourself available to answer questions. When the task is complete, evaluate the outcome with the person. Praise a competent job and make suggestions for improvement in areas that are not up to your expectations.

10. **Get Help From Outside Experts** — Most nonprofits require a network of support in order to operate effectively. Many small organizations use a board recruitment process that ensures the availability of professional expertise in key areas. Large or more mature nonprofits may strive to build a staff that includes experts in various professional disciplines. While board members can bring tremendous insight and wisdom to a nonprofit based on their professional backgrounds, and full-time professional experts can enhance your operations, there are at least three disciplines where the use of independent, outside professional advisors is almost always appropriate: legal, accounting and insurance. The principal reason for using outside experts in the accounting and insurance areas is the potential for differing interests. Yet there is a more practical reason: for many nonprofits, it is more cost-effective to use outside experts than to maintain in-house staff to meet occasional as opposed to ongoing needs. In addition, outside advisors with other similar clients may have access to networks, as well as broad expertise that can benefit your agency.

11. **Inventory Assets** — It is important to conduct an inventory of vital assets as part of an ongoing risk management effort because it might be impossible to do so in the aftermath of a crisis. What assets? Consider *intangible* assets first. Keep in mind that, while you could probably operate without some of your office equipment, once your reputation has hit the skids, continuing may be impossible. Next, move on to tangible assets. Consider all of the property, both on and off premises, you need and use to achieve your mission. If you returned to your building tomorrow and discovered it was uninhabitable, would you be able to recall the number of telephones, filing cabinets, CPUs and the equipment previously used to deliver services? Assuming you have insurance to cover your losses, a detailed inventory that survives the fire, flood or other disaster will make the work with claims adjusters less painful.

Additional pieces of important information include whether the property is owned or leased, and relevant identifying information, such as brand names, model names or numbers, serial numbers, lessors, leasing agreement numbers — all the details you require for replacement or remuneration.

If your facility includes office, as well as service delivery equipment (recreational or playground equipment, a computer learning center or medical equipment), you might develop separate inventories based on the different uses of your facility. Critical records should also be inventoried. These include insurance forms; leases; partnership agreements; and client, volunteer and funder databases. You will need copies on site for reference and use; backup copies should be kept off site in a lock box or in your attorney's office. Wherever possible, use existing sources of information to compile your inventory, such as an up-to-date fixed assets schedule.

12. **Comply With Applicable Local, State and Federal Regulations** — Child labor laws; Fair Labor Standards Act; Americans with Disabilities Act; permits to run a day-care center; licenses for staff (employee and volunteer) professionals; inspection/ maintenance certificates. Beyond the general legal principles and broad statutes that apply to every person and organization (including your nonprofit), each particular kind of business activity is governed by highly detailed regulations that are issued and enforced by the local, state and federal governments that have jurisdiction wherever your nonprofit operates. Collectively, these regulations are the basis for what is known as *regulatory* or *administrative* law — comparable to, and just as important as, the more widely understood contract, tort, and criminal branches of the law.

Thus, a nonprofit child-care center that is located in a particular town and a national nonprofit that focuses on combating a given disease will both be governed by the same laws that apply to everyone, but each of these two nonprofits also must comply with vastly different regulations. These differences arise from the differences in the two organizations' respective activities, in the constituencies they serve, in the geographical areas where they operate, and in the sources and uses of their funds. Because of these differences, every nonprofit is subject to a virtually unique set of regulations. Furthermore, these regulations usually are very detailed and are revised frequently by the federal, state, and local authorities who are responsible for enforcing them. Therefore, the managers of each nonprofit need to not only learn and fulfill the requirements of the regulations that govern their specific activities; these managers also must stay abreast of changes in these regulations and must recognize that these regulations may differ from state to state, or even between counties or towns. Failure to know and comply with regulatory requirements can be just as crippling to a nonprofit's activities as a violation of criminal law.

13. **Implement Workable Internal Controls** — Much of what many nonprofits are already doing with respect to tracking, accounting for and protecting financial assets likely falls within one of four categories of internal controls:

❑ *authorization and approval* — activities empowering a person to sanction expenditures, including policies and a sign-off system;

❑ *proper documentation* — activities creating a paper trail of the nonprofit's revenue stream and spending, including the accounting routines created to track money coming in and going out;

❑ *physical security* — protective measures that safeguard assets by preventing theft by insiders or outsiders, as well as preventing access to accounting systems by those whose positions do not require access; and

❑ *early detection* — any activity that could detect a fraudulent scheme in the planning or execution stage and enable intervention to stop the scheme and prevent the further erosion of assets.

Fortunately, establishing good internal controls requires more of an investment of attention than money. Thus very small nonprofits or even all-volunteer groups, as well as large, secular and religious umbrella organizations can institute appropriate controls and reap the benefits.

14. **Prepare to Pay for Some Accidental Losses** — Despite all these safety measures, some accidents are going to strike virtually every nonprofit from time to time: some property may be damaged, some people (clients, employees, volunteers, even some officers of your nonprofit) may suffer injuries, and someone may threaten a lawsuit. A well-managed nonprofit must be prepared for, and not surprised by, the expenditures that these accidents and claims inevitably bring. Some of the smaller, more probable accident costs should be included in your budget. For larger, less predictable accident expenses and claims, a forward-looking, mission-focused nonprofit must arrange appropriate financing.

15. **Communicate Regularly With Stakeholders** — Stakeholders are persons and organizations who are *invested* in the nonprofit in some way. Stockholders are stakeholders of a company. Clients, volunteers, employees, board members, partners, parent/ umbrella organizations, individual donors, foundation and corporate funders, the local community, government agencies, and the general public are stakeholders of a community-serving nonprofit.

Communicating your vision of the future to your stakeholders increases the odds of their cooperation in and support of your endeavors. Their understanding of and enthusiasm for the plans could entice new funders, new volunteers, and new clients while increasing the organization's standing in the community. All of which are upside risks. On the flip side, keeping stakeholders in the dark can backfire and create great downside risk to your reputation with attendant financial, people and property losses.

Keeping stakeholders apprised of your plans can also quell fears or concerns and inspire confidence in your organization. For example, rumor may have it that your doors are closing or that your organization is so flush it no longer requires individual donations to stay afloat. Neither vision of the future would be advantageous for your mission. However, stakeholders privy to your plans to accommodate twice as many clients next year or who understand your bottom line would not be shaken by this news and could do a lot to assuage the rumors in the community.

Your goal is to keep stakeholders wedded to your mission. By keeping them in the loop, you validate that they made a good choice by investing in your organization.

Step 4 — Act on Your Decision

This step follows the logical progression of the strategic risk management process, from conceptual to specific, from a wide swath of context analysis, to a list of specific action steps the organization will take to protect its core assets and take advantage of opportunities.

As an organization proceeds to implement a strategic risk management program, it is a good idea to keep the following guiding principles in mind:

❑ *Practical, not protracted* — Where a practical, straightforward approach is available and is expected to yield the same result as a more technical approach, choose the practical. A complicated policy about the types of locations where a tutoring program may be held might be unnecessary when a requirement that tutoring be held at one of the branches of the public library addresses the nonprofit's concern about the isolation of vulnerable clients.

❑ *Consider people first* — Try to involve the persons most affected by a strategic risk management strategy in its design. After gaining experience implementing a wide range of risk management techniques, you will have ample evidence that the people required to follow the policy, install the security measures, train the lifeguards, and screen the applicants, will be your most creative problem-solvers. Even more rewarding, they will champion the new policy they helped craft.

❑ *Do not assume* — Be sure to confirm that someone obtained a valid license to hold the 10K event, ordered refreshments for the participants (and the crowd), and arranged for ambulances to be standing by. When working in a collaborative way with another organization, it is sound risk management to put into writing what each organization is committing to do, by when, for how much money and who is liable if any of this goes wrong.

❑ *Use common sense before dollars and cents* — In many cases, you will find that a common sense approach works more effectively and offers a better solution than one costing next year's fund-raising proceeds. Few nonprofits need the kind of video surveillance security systems that are standard fare at Las Vegas casinos. However a sound Technology Policy providing advance consent in writing by the employee for periodic monitoring of e-mail and Web traffic can effectively dissuade staff from using your Internet connection for illegal, unethical or inappropriate purposes.

Step 5 — Follow up and Adjust

Few nonprofits describe their operations as stagnant. Most report that they are constantly seeking and evaluating new opportunities to positively change the lives of their clients or the health of a community. This constant state of flux in the nonprofit necessitates a continuing review of strategic risk management strategies to make certain they remain viable and appropriate given the new circumstances facing the organization. Abandon techniques that have proven futile, have cost the nonprofit more than the expected or that are simply no longer appropriate given the new environment. Consider changes, adjustments and revisions anytime the technique serving an important purpose is not as effective as it might be.

Summary

This chapter presented the five-step Strategic Risk Management Process as a foundation on which an organization can construct a strategic risk management program. Thoughtful consideration of the organization's resources and environment is the important first step. Appraising risks — identifying and then ranking risks — is the next step. The cycle continues with identifying risk management techniques (Decide What to Do), implementing these techniques (Act on Your Decision), and monitoring their effectiveness and making adjustments as necessary (Follow up and Adjust). A literature search on the topic of risk management would reveal at least a dozen variations on this process. Yet all of the approaches to capturing risk management as a series of steps seem to share the never-ending characteristic. Given the role of risk management in your nonprofit — more akin to a daily vitamin than a powerful antibiotic taken over a 5-day period — the most important advice we can offer now is to encourage the formulation of a plan. Get started. Begin with a modest program that addresses priority risks in one or two key areas of operations. Build support from within the organization, so that the outcomes of the process earn support from those who will have to adhere to new rules or teach others to do so. Start gradually and construct a program that will fortify your nonprofit for its lifetime.

Risk Control for Maximum Benefit

T he goal of this chapter is to explore practical opportunities for nonprofits to use procedural and management controls to reduce threats of accidental losses.

Accidents have been a part of the human experience since time immemorial. Yet despite our centuries-old experience with them, human beings today still struggle to understand the causes of accidents and use this understanding to prevent unexpected and unintended events that cause loss. Although we do not fully understand why accidents occur, our attempts to explain them remain the most logical launching pad for a discussion about preventing them.

Several established theories about accident causation are potentially illuminating as we explore how a nonprofit can use information about its own practices and experience to reduce the probability and severity of accidents involving the organization's premises or participants. We discuss three of these theories. Each of them potentially applies to any of the accidents we will be mentioning, and each theory about how an accident was caused leads to its own set of measures for preventing similar future accidents. Having a variety of prevention measures from which to choose lets you select the ones that make the most sense within your nonprofit.

■ **The Domino Theory** – H.W. Heinrich, an early 20th century industrial safety engineer, developed the *domino theory* of accident causation as a way of explaining that accidents result when a chain of events occurs. According to Heinrich, a chain of five conditions and/or events precede accidents occurring in the workplace and society:

1. ancestry and social environment,

2. the fault of a person,

3. an unsafe act and/or mechanical or physical danger,

4. the accident itself, and

5. the resulting injury.

According to Heinrich, an accident can be prevented by simply removing any one of the events or conditions that precede the actual accident. His theory continues by positing that the most effective way to prevent a resulting injury is to address number 3: avoiding the unsafe act or removing the danger.

Despite a wide range of strategies intended to eliminate the chance of a fatal injury, every year a number of community-based youth recreation facilities with swimming pools experience an accidental drowning. A closer review of these terrible events points to the need for rigorous training of lifeguards as the best way to prevent these accidents. Applying the domino theory, the most effective way to prevent a drowning death would be to remove the danger itself: the swimming pool. Yet many of these centers provide the only available place for inner-city youth to learn to swim and enjoy the benefits of this sport. Unwilling to remove what could be regarded as a danger by some and the heart and soul of the program by others, recreation programs focus on addressing the other elements in the chain of dominos by:

❑ teaching swim safety to program participants (changing the social environment of the pool);

❑ disciplining or removing swimmers whose behavior endangers others at the pool (preventing unsafe acts);

❑ firing lifeguards whose conduct falls below standard (more unsafe acts);

❑ installing non-slip surfaces in areas near the pool (a dangerous condition); and

❑ developing procedures for transporting pool-accident victims to hospitals if needed (reducing the resulting injury).

■ **General Methods of Control** — A second theory of accident causation emerged subsequent to the domino theory. This theory, called the General Methods of Control approach, holds that unsafe physical conditions, rather than careless or otherwise unsafe human actions, are the principal cause of accidents in the workplace. Under this theory, there are 11 general ways to control industrial accidents and diseases:

1. *Substitution of a less harmful material for one that is more dangerous to health.* For example, a nonprofit daycare center may decide to use an herbal cleaning solution instead of one containing a combination of harsh chemicals after it learns of a report linking childhood allergies to the chemical mix.

2. *Change or alteration of a process to minimize worker contact.* An elementary school may decide to clean rather than paint a small storage area due to the school's concern that the combination of paint fumes and poor ventilation is too dangerous for the maintenance crew.

3. *Isolation or enclosure of a process or work operation to reduce the number of persons exposed.* A nonprofit performing arts center may decide to remodel its auditorium during the program's month-long winter recess to reduce the number of people who will be exposed to dust and debris from the construction.

4. *Wet methods to reduce generation of dust in operations.* Traditionally developed in mining and quarrying, this method is equally important in controlling flying dust that may injure the eyes of youngsters playing baseball during hot, dry summers or construction-related dust affecting volunteers at a home construction site.

5. *Local exhaust at the point of generation and dispersion of contaminants.* This is a concern not only in industrial settings but also in public lavatories in many of the facilities where nonprofits conduct or sponsor community events.

6. *General or dilution ventilation with clean air to provide a more healthful atmosphere.* An adult day-care center has the HVAC (heating, ventilation and air conditioning) system retrofitted to introduce filtered outside air into the building to increase the amount of oxygen in this renovated, tightly sealed environment.

7. *Personal protective devices such as special clothing, eye and respiratory protection.* A community-based program that builds homes for low-income residents issues protective gear to the volunteers who sign up to help with various tasks on the construction site.

8. *Good housekeeping, including cleanliness of the workplace, waste disposal, adequate washing and eating facilities, healthful drinking water, and control of insects and rodents.* A soup kitchen signs a long-term contract with a pest control company whereby the company conducts thorough monthly inspections and undertakes pest control treatments as necessary.

9. *Special control methods for specific dangers.* A parent in a custody dispute attempts to enter a family recreation center where her daughter is playing basketball. Because she does not have the correct badge, she is denied access and the child's kidnapping is aborted.

10. *Medical programs to detect intake of toxic materials.* A blood bank installs carbon monoxide detectors in strategic locations at its headquarters.

11. *Training and education to supplement engineering controls.* The purpose is to make people more aware of perhaps hidden dangers and the steps to take after an accident to prevent further harm. A nonprofit community beautification organization trains its volunteers how to prune tree branches without inadvertently cutting themselves or others. Another part of the training alerts the volunteers to the presence and use of the first-aid kit that every pruning group is instructed to carry. Another lesson indicates proper lengths to cut pruned branches and how to stack in the safest manner for pick up.

Under the General Methods of Control approach, loss prevention activities focus on controlling physical forces and conditions, rather then preventing human error.

- **System Safety Approach** — According to this theory, an accident is likely to occur when a component of a larger system of interconnected parts and processes fails to work as intended. The System Safety Approach calls for the analysis of systems and operations according to the following steps:

  1. *The identification of dangers.* For example, a tour of a facility that will be used for child care, as well as family counseling, might reveal that the bathrooms in the building are unsuitable for children because stalls contain floor-to-ceiling doors, and potentially dangerous appliances or electrical equipment are located in areas that will be accessible by children.

  2. *The timely incorporation of effective safety-related design and operational specifications.* Using the previous example, the nonprofit purchaser of the facility may decide to renovate the facility, creating kid-friendly bathrooms that enable staff to observe children coming and going, incorporating a separate utility room, and designing a kitchen with a counter that makes it very difficult for young clients to reach appliances and outlets.

  3. *The early evaluation of design and procedures for compliance with safety requirements and criteria.* The renovation plans are reviewed by safety experts, as well as specialists in the construction of facilities serving children.

  4. *The ongoing monitoring of safety aspects of the system or operation.* Periodic inspections of the renovated facility are conducted to make certain that its kid-friendly and safety features are working as intended. Equipment and furniture are routinely inspected, maintained, repaired or replaced.

Risk Control Techniques: Where the Rubber Hits the Road

Every nonprofit has an unlimited palette of risk control techniques from which it can choose the strategies that best suit the organization.

Techniques that suit an organization are likely to be those that:

❑ the nonprofit can afford to implement,

❑ the nonprofit can train its paid and volunteer staff to administer,

❑ will be understood and supported by a diverse group of stakeholders, from 20-year veterans on the staff to spontaneous volunteers,

❑ do not cost more than the corresponding loss they are intended to prevent, and

❑ do not require the nonprofit to deviate from its core mission or values.

Just as a painter relies on a foundation of three primary colors (red, yellow and blue) to form every other color under the rainbow, a risk manager relies on a foundation of five risk-control techniques to form strategies for every conceivable situation. When thinking about how to approach any given danger, start with these five categories of risk control measures to help you or your nonprofit's risk management committee view a wide range of alternatives.

1. *Avoidance* — When a nonprofit avoids a risk it does something to reduce the probability of a loss to zero. Choosing avoidance is suitable whenever the *expected* value of losses is greater than the *expected* value of benefits the nonprofit will derive from undertaking a particular activity. The nonprofit may decide to avoid a specific aspect of its programs, or not to conduct an activity altogether. For example, a scouting organization may decide to postpone a camping trip after hurricane-strength winds are forecast. The same scouting group may decide to sponsor a magazine subscription sale instead of a series of bake sales after the local television station airs a story on food safety and food poisoning.

2. *Loss Prevention* — When a nonprofit takes steps to reduce the probability or frequency of a loss, without eliminating its possibility altogether, it is practicing loss prevention. For example, a nonprofit's audit firm advises the executive director to receive unopened monthly bank statements from the person processing the mail and review these statements thoroughly. The executive director looks for any unusual endorsements, verifies that all payees are legitimate vendors of the nonprofit, and checks that her signature appears on the cancelled checks. Doing so does not eliminate the possibility of a fraud loss. But the process may dissuade staff from attempting to embezzle the organization's funds. It also reduces the chance of a continuing fraud, such as checks for a relatively small amount being written to a dummy vendor on a monthly basis.

3. *Loss Reduction* — When a nonprofit practices loss reduction, it takes steps to reduce the magnitude of a loss that occurs despite efforts to prevent it. These can be divided into *pre-loss measures* that are applied

before a loss occurs and *post-loss measures* that are invoked directly after a loss. A nonprofit that operates a skateboard park as part of its community-based family recreation and cultural center may require that skaters don protective helmets and kneepads prior to entering the park. A nonprofit association may have a policy that no more than two managers may take the same flight. The safety gear probably does not change the probability that a skater will lose control of his board. Requiring senior managers to take different flights does nothing to improve the safety of the various aircraft used to transport the team. Yet, if a skater falls off his board, the helmet and kneepads are likely to reduce the severity of the injury. If one of the planes on which the association's managers are traveling crashes, the organization will not have lost its entire management team. Post-loss measures for these two examples might include the nonprofit requiring that a stocked first-aid kit and at least two first-aid-certified staff be on duty when the skate park is open. The nonprofit association might make arrangements with a counseling service to provide immediate assistance to family members of employees, in the event an employee is injured or killed at work. The agreement negotiated in advance of an emergency will save time and may enable the nonprofit to avoid a lawsuit by demonstrating its caring and concern for the families of victims.

> **F**ew nonprofits can afford to have a fully programmed but idle network server on standby in the event the nonprofit's principal server malfunctions. But many organizations can afford the cost of a subscription to a Web-based service that acts as a temporary information-technology hot-site should the nonprofit's server fail.

4.   ***Segregation of Exposure Units*** — This technique calls for either separating a nonprofit's assets or some aspect of its operations, or creating a reserve unit or process (a Plan B) that is only used when the primary asset or process is rendered inaccessible or inoperable. Duplication of assets is generally regarded as a luxury few nonprofits can afford. But a closer look suggests that this technique can be adapted to increase its affordability. For example, having a separate furnished facility available to house clients in the event a fire necessitates the closing of the headquarters facility is impractical. But entering into a cooperative arrangement with a sister agency in the community that would enable the transfer of the nonprofit's clients to the sister agency's facility on a temporary basis is a workable solution. It serves the interests of both organizations to work out the arrangement long before an event requires use of the other's facility. For another case in point, few nonprofits can afford to have a fully programmed but idle network server on standby in the event the nonprofit's principal server malfunctions. But many organizations can afford the cost of a subscription to a Web-based service that acts as a temporary information-technology hot-site should the nonprofit's server fail.

5. ***Contractual Sharing for Risk Control*** — A nonprofit can enter into a contract that shifts responsibility for losses to another party. Unlike contractual sharing for risk financing (discussed in Chapter 1), contractual sharing for risk control does not involve an indemnification agreement, whereby one party agrees to pay the legal costs (*indemnify*) of another. For example, a nonprofit recreation organization politely declines the offer of a group of parents to install playground equipment over a surface that meets Consumer Product Safety Commission playground standards, and instead hires a contractor. The contractor is responsible for obtaining workers' compensation coverage for his work crew, thus removing this responsibility from the nonprofit. The nonprofit could still suffer a loss if the equipment fails or a client sustains a serious injury due to the failure of the surface, but arguably it has shared some of the exposure related to the proper installation of the playground with the contractor. It is important to note that contractual sharing for risk transfer is never equivalent to risk avoidance: using the playground example, the risk of a fall has not been eliminated.

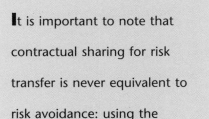

It is important to note that contractual sharing for risk transfer is never equivalent to risk avoidance: using the playground example, the risk of a fall has not been eliminated.

Summary

When a nonprofit understands why and how accidents occur in its facilities and during the course of service delivery, it is in a stronger position to avoid these accidents altogether or reduce their frequency and magnitude.

Most nonprofits use a combination of risk control techniques — exposure avoidance, loss prevention, loss reduction, segregation of exposure units, and contractual sharing for risk control — while considering their unique circumstances and available resources. The combination of techniques and strategies that will be appropriate in a particular nonprofit is unlikely to work as effectively in another organization. Thus, each organization must decide for itself what course will empower the nonprofit and support its efforts to fulfill its community-serving mission.

CHAPTER 5

What's Nonprofit Got to Do With It?

For at least the past several decades, nonprofit managers and executives have been repeatedly admonished to adopt business practices. "Run your nonprofit like a business," is the mantra of well-intentioned gurus, several of whom have enjoyed success as authors of best-selling paperback how-to management books. Yet for many effective and successful nonprofit managers this simple advice ignores the tremendous management skills of seasoned nonprofit managers and executives, many of whom have devoted their entire careers to the nonprofit world. After all, the more than 1.5 million nonprofits that make up the nonprofit world collectively represent the fastest growing sector in the U.S. economy. And a closer examination of the nonprofit sector reveals a collection of tremendously diverse organizations that face enormous odds on a daily basis and are run with admirable skill and leadership.

Add to this mix the issue of risk. Managing risk is confusing to many nonprofits. They receive conflicting signals. The business-oriented texts that include mention of risk management admonish nonprofits to eliminate risk. Yet the seasoned nonprofit manager knows that risk taking is lifeblood of an organization dedicated to improving the lives of the poor, revitalizing a community, advocating for people without a voice, or supporting environmental protection in opposition to hundreds of millions of dollars in corporate profits.

Throughout this book we have borrowed, adapted and interpreted traditional risk management theories, concepts and strategies that were born in the business world to cope with threats of *unforeseen accidental losses*. Embracing but going beyond these traditional practices, we have focused on enhancing nonprofits' resources when our uncertain world gives us opportunities for gain. Now we will take another path. We will examine some of the unique aspects of nonprofit organizations for which there is no corresponding corporate model. Along this path, we will once again be managing risk strategically: both reducing threats of accidental loss and, where appropriate, remaining alert for opportunities to achieve surprising gains in these special nonprofit activities.

Volunteers: The Inexplicable Resource

One of the most important characteristics that distinguish nonprofit from for-profit organizations is the presence of volunteers. At a minimum, most nonprofits have a volunteer leadership team, its board of directors. Beyond that, anything goes. An organization may employ a handful, several hundred or several thousand volunteers. Some nonprofits spend a long time recruiting a small cadre of volunteers for long-term assignments, such as one-to-one mentoring of at-risk youth, while others quickly enroll hundreds or thousands to help with disaster relief efforts or to staff a large one-day public event. Volunteers come from all walks of life. Nonprofits deploy volunteers in traditional professions, from doctors and nurses to lawyers and accountants, as well as individuals with specialized training, such as massage therapists, athletic coaches and foster parents.

An estimated 83.9 billion people volunteer on an annual basis, contributing more than 15.5 billion hours. The contributions of America's volunteers are difficult to measure, although one organization has put the price tag at $239 billion, representing the equivalent of more than 9 million full-time employees. As is true with other endeavors, sometimes the best-laid plans do not work out the way you intended. With respect to volunteers, every nonprofit should consider the possibility that:

- A volunteer will suffer an injury while serving a nonprofit.

- A volunteer will cause injury to the clients of a nonprofit, either from an accident or intentional wrongdoing.

- A volunteer will damage the nonprofit's reputation or do something that will threaten the assets of the organization.

None of these is reason to avoid volunteer-associated risks by relying solely on paid staff. Without volunteers most nonprofits would be hamstrung in their efforts to bring positive change to a community or client population.

Instead, a thoughtful approach to volunteer risk management is in order. We offer the following suggestions for getting a handle on the risks that arise when volunteer staff members are deployed in a nonprofit.

1. ***Design Volunteer Positions With Care*** — No nonprofit organization can afford to bring on a single volunteer without first giving thought to the role the volunteer will play in the organization, the supervision the individual will receive, and the rules that will apply to the volunteer. Failing to take the time for these steps is a recipe for disaster.

2. ***Train, Teach, Coach*** — Some volunteers come to an organization with extraordinary skills and seasoned professionalism. Yet it is very rare that a volunteer will be doing the same work in the same environment as his or her principal profession. For example, a nonprofit might send teams of doctors and nurses to a war-torn, third-world country. Although the teams are trauma specialists, it is unlikely they will have experience exercising their professional skills in facilities without air conditioning or running water.

3. ***Supervise*** — Volunteer orientation programs have come of age during the past 20 plus years. The vast majority of nonprofits recognize that it is important to provide an orientation to all newcomers, that includes volunteers. Yet some of the same organizations neglect to spend enough time honing the supervisory rules and practices that apply.

4. ***Remove as Needed*** — From time to time it becomes necessary to remove a volunteer because continued service poses a danger to the nonprofit or its service recipients. The need to remove a poor-performing volunteer may be complicated by the fact that the volunteer is also a long-time donor, works for a local media outlet, has friends on the nonprofit's board, and other potentially downside risk scenarios. The key is to consider the possibility of removal before such action is required. Every nonprofit with volunteer staff should have a plan for addressing volunteer misbehavior. The plan should incorporate discipline, while considering the possibility that removal may be required in rare instances.

As for upside risks that offer unexpected opportunities for growth of your volunteer force, look for ways to:

1. ***Find Innovative Sources of Volunteers.*** Perhaps your nonprofit provides a service where those who have been clients often graduate to become qualified as excellent, understanding volunteers or even paid staff. This could certainly be true for adult literacy programs, teen reproductive health programs, or other mentoring settings. Those who have learned and realize the practical daily value of their new knowledge often are the most inspiring teachers and role models.

Excellent volunteers may come from surprising sources of seemingly idle people — for example, inmates of minimum-security prisons or residents of assisted-living facilities. Does your nonprofit need some tasks performed that some of these often-eager people could do, either on your premises or with clients or materials your staff could take to them?

2. **Promote From Within.** Does your nonprofit regularly promote from within — where some clients can hope to become volunteers, some volunteers employees, some employees managers, and some managers members of advisory committees or even the board? Serving as a loyal volunteer can be the start of a satisfying career for persons truly dedicated to your mission.

3. **Recruit Celebrity Volunteers.** Be ready for that one most surprising day when a celebrity, even a local one, makes some contact with your nonprofit. Opportunity is pounding down your door if a national media celebrity or professional sports star happens to telephone or visit your facilities. Opportunity still is knocking if the call or visit is from a local news anchor or talk-show host. Welcome such special people. If they express personal interest in your nonprofit's work, urge them to become a volunteer. They will bring others, especially if you can mention them in your publicity. Others will come — they want to be "Like Mike."

Fundraising: Money for Nothing

With rare exceptions, most nonprofits are in the fund-raising business. In fact, without fund-raising activities, few organizations could generate sufficient funding to support their community-serving activities. Fund-raising activities are fraught with risk, including the upside risk of receiving more donations than the organization is prepared to handle, and the downside, more familiar, risk of receiving less money than the goal of a fund-raising campaign.

Despite its risky nature, fundraising rarely receives adequate attention by the risk management committee. And it is not unusual for the downsides of fundraising to be overlooked altogether. Below are some guiding principles that every nonprofit should consider as it strives to minimize the downside risks of fundraising and maximize the upside risks.

1. **Develop a Gift Acceptance Policy** — An increasingly popular strategy for confronting the possibility of an inappropriate gift is to develop a gift-acceptance strategy that sets forth the nonprofit's criteria for gifts. These policies were first seen in the

cultural arts community, where the need to identify suitable items is paramount. A recent article in the *Chronicle of Philanthropy* titled "Treasure Trove or Trash Bin" reported on the range of unusual gifts offered to nonprofits in recent years. From questionable works of art to scripts from 70s-era TV shows, to antique automobiles to homes sitting atop leaking underground storage tanks, there is no shortage of would-be philanthropists anxious to obtain a tax write-off on unwanted collections. A gift-acceptance policy is a handy reference the nonprofit can provide anyone interested in making a donation, as well as a set of guiding principles that the leadership of the organization can refer to in determining whether to accept a gift. A key consideration in such a policy is whether the item is one that the organization can choose to use right away or discard if and when it likes (versus a gift that requires the recipient to maintain it for a long period). Circumstances change often in the nonprofit sector and only a small percentage of nonprofits are in position to retain gifts over a long period. While each organization needs to examine its resources, mission and plans for the future in crafting a gift-acceptance policy that will be appropriate, we offer the following as a sample:

S A M P L E

Gift Acceptance Policy

1.   [Name of Nonprofit] solicits and accepts gifts that are consistent with its mission and that support its core programs, as well as special projects.

2.   Donations and other forms of support will generally be accepted from individuals, partnerships, corporations, foundations, government agencies, or other entities, subject to the following limitations:

> a. [describe limitations here, such as delivered to the agency, new or nearly new condition, proof of ownership.]

3.   Gifts of Real Property, Personal Property or Securities may only be accepted upon approval of the [name of appropriate reviewing body, such as the nonprofit's Finance Committee].

2.   ***Get It in Writing*** — Corporate gifts are a vital source of revenue for countless nonprofits. These gifts may originate from the philanthropic arm of the organization (a corporate foundation or an amount of profits set aside for gifts to charity), or they may be

dollars from the marketing budget. Twenty years ago, many corporate gifts were made with little expectation of tangible return to the business. The company's name may have appeared on the banner at the road race, or a company spokesperson was featured on the dais at the fund-raising dinner. Much has changed in recent years. It is not uncommon for a corporation to make requests of the nonprofit in the weeks after the generous donation check has been cashed. Inquiries about vacancies on the board of directors or other perceived benefits of affiliation may arise. Nonprofit CEOs and development professionals need to be prepared to respond to these requests for favors in the wake of a donation. How will the nonprofit respond?

One approach to consider is memorializing the terms of a corporate donation in writing and having the document signed by both organizations. Like an informal grant agreement, the document acknowledges the receipt of funds and outlines any restriction on their use (to support the construction of the new child-care wing at the family recreation center). The development of the document may give the corporation the opportunity it needs to make certain requests of the nonprofit.

3. ***Monitor Restricted Grants With Care*** — In the excitement following the award of a restricted grant from a private or public foundation, a nonprofit may overlook the stringent deadlines and reporting requirements that are attached to the grant. This is particularly true in small- to mid-sized organizations without a full-time development office and experienced grants managers. In many respects, restricted grants are actually liabilities to a nonprofit until the grant restrictions have been met and the specter of having to return the money to the funder (after it has been spent) dissipates. During the last decade there have been several widely publicized suits against nonprofits by donors alleging that a nonprofit recipient did not spend the money in the way the donor intended. While the courts continue to give nonprofits more than a few chances, such as by granting time extensions before allowing a suit to proceed, there is no question that if a nonprofit refuses to honor the restrictions on a gift or grant, a court will intervene in a civil suit filed by the donor and require that the money be returned.

4. ***Be Prepared to Reject an Inappropriate Fund-raising Scheme*** — In the world of nonprofit fundraising, there is no place for a philosophy that focuses only on the dollars raised and not the methods of raising them. From time to time, your nonprofit may be approached by a well-intentioned supporter who wants to raise money for your organization in a manner that would be inappropriate or potentially embarrassing.

Whether the event has the potential to cause serious harm to participants or your reputation, you must weigh the threats and opportunities and decide what is in the best interest of your nonprofit. For example, an animal rights group might decide that a charitable foxhunt is an inappropriate fundraiser, while a local historic preservation society might regard the event as acceptable. And you need to be prepared to explain your decision.

5. ***Be Ready on the Upside for Your Gift From Heaven*** — Just in case a surprise donor or foundation wants to offer a true, unrestricted fortune to your nonprofit, perhaps some multiple of your annual budget, have a general plan prepared, ideally in writing, to answer the question: How will you spend the money? While your response needs to be flexible to meet the benefactor's purposes, also be prepared to expand your overall mission — in terms of the clientele, the geographic area or economic sectors you serve, even your vision of the ways your nonprofit betters the world — to be ready with an intelligent, thoughtful answer. Indeed, your board's thinking carefully about how they *would* spend the money if they actually had it often opens the members' minds to new possibilities, visions, plans, and eventual realities, for growth.

6. ***Always Send a Prompt, Written Thank-You Letter*** — Acknowledging a gift, no matter how small, is an inexpensive way to keep the door open for consideration the next time you submit a proposal. Thank the funder for supporting your mission with the grant or donation, briefly summarize how this money (or item) will benefit the community or your clients, and invite the funder to visit the facility or attend an upcoming event (not the fundraiser) to see your nonprofit in action.

Resource Constraints: The Ties That Bind

Many businesses operate in a cycle that includes good times and bad. Good times are evident in generous bonuses and employee benefits of onsite health club privileges and periodic visits by massage therapists. The bad times might be characterized by downsizing, relocating the organization to a distant suburb, and the elimination of perks that have long been taken for granted. While some nonprofits face similar cycles of feast and famine, a much more common situation is the ever-present resource-constrained environment. Why do so many nonprofits operate under circumstances where there are never enough resources to achieve the organization's goals? A closer look at the mission of typical community-serving nonprofits provides a hint at the answer:

- "eliminating poverty in New York City,"

- "providing a safe place to live for poor residents of this city,"

- "helping underprivileged school children improve their academic performance and obtain admission to the college of their choosing."

The missions of most nonprofits are enormously ambitious. Nonprofits seek to change communities, transform the lives of persons ignored by government programs and draw attention to the misdeeds of big business. Others strive to cure disease, fund life-saving treatments for patients without financial resources, or groom the next generation of leaders.

Given this environment of continuing challenge to stay afloat and realize an impossible mission, how can risk management help? Examining both the upside risks (unanticipated funding) and downside risks (a financial crisis), before they materialize can help a nonprofit make strategic choices today and prepare for an uncertain future. In Chapter 3 we laid out a five-step risk management process. If an organization seeks to integrate strategic risk management into its operations, it should consider factors that might heighten or ease the resource-constrained environment, such as:

❑ the indication by a long-term funder that its priorities have moved to an area outside the mission of the nonprofit;

❑ the ongoing mergers and consolidations of firms that constitute a major donor base for the nonprofit, resulting in fewer donors over time;

❑ the decision of a government funder to put its contracts for services out to bid, versus awarding sole source contracts to the nonprofit;

❑ the decision of a major public foundation to devote 10 percent of its grant-making dollars to research in the area of the nonprofit's specialty; and

❑ the interest by members of a community in supporting the cause of a nonprofit following the recruitment of a celebrity spokesperson.

Whatever the circumstances, a nonprofit should consider what, if anything, it can do to minimize the possible negative outcomes and maximize the possible positive outcomes. What steps can and should it take now, and what can and should it do if circumstances unfold in a way that is not advantageous to the nonprofit?

Once in a Lifetime

A growing number of nonprofits sponsor once-in-a-lifetime activities, from rallies attracting tens of thousands of participants, to large-scale fund-raising events. On the upside, these events have the potential to attract enormous numbers of supporters, raise to new heights awareness about the nonprofit's cause, and generate funding that can be used for operational expenses during the lean months of the program year.

Yet the very nature of these events — the large crowds, the media attention, and the need for legions of volunteers — heightens the risk they pose to the sponsor. There are a number of practical risk management strategies every nonprofit sponsoring a once-in-a-lifetime event should consider. These include:

1. ***Form a Safety Committee*** — Through the simple act of naming a safety committee as part of the planning group for a special event, a nonprofit ups the odds that potentially harmful incidents can be avoided. As is true with any risk management committee, diversity is key to ensure a good mix of viewpoints and perspectives. While there are numerous tasks that must be tended to in planning the event, the safety committee can devote its full attention to helping the organization plan and execute the event with a high degree of safety.

2. ***Collaborate With Care*** — Every major special event sponsored by a nonprofit involves countless partnerships and collaborations. Partners may include firms and agencies providing donated goods and services, the local police force that will coordinate with the nonprofit to determine public safety considerations, and the vendors who will sell their wares to the members of the general public attending the event. In all cases it is critical that the nonprofit strive for clarity in communicating its expectations and requirements. Never assume that because a partner, vendor or collaborator is an established business, large corporation or prominent nonprofit that the organization is in someway protecting your nonprofit against losses. If you require that partners carry certain limits of liability insurance, require also that certificates of insurance be provided. In most cases, a written agreement outlining the terms of the partnership or involvement is an invaluable risk management tool. During the process of negotiating the agreement, many issues will come to light and the parties to the agreement will have the opportunity to thoughtfully assign duties and responsibilities, including responsibility for losses that occur despite the best efforts of all involved.

3. ***Review the Insurance Program*** — It is important to speak with your insurance professional (agent, broker or consultant) about your plans for a once-in-a-lifetime event. Do not assume that because it is an important activity for your nonprofit, that your current policies will automatically provide coverage. If the event is both unusual and one that would not generally be offered by a nonprofit such as yours, you may need to purchase separate coverage for the event. The key is discussing the upcoming event with your insurance professional as soon as it is a twinkle in your eye. As the event nears, it will be more difficult to obtain coverage.

Many Masters

The corporate accounting scandals of 2002 drew unprecedented attention to the importance of accountability to stakeholders, including shareholders and employees. Nonprofits, like their business counterparts, must strive to be accountable to various stakeholders. Stakeholders are persons and organizations who are invested in the nonprofit in some way. But unlike private businesses, the number of organizations and individuals to whom nonprofits must be accountable is staggering. These publics include:

- Clients

- Volunteers

- Employees

- The general public

- Individual donors

- Foundation and corporate funders

- Government agencies, including funders and regulators

- Partners, including nonprofits, businesses and government agencies

- Parent and umbrella organizations

- The community in which the nonprofit operates

Given this diverse and potentially enormous array of stakeholders, nonprofits must be particularly diligent and watchful of accountability issues. Some guiding strategic risk management principles for accountability include:

1. ***Strive to Conduct the Nonprofit's Business in a Manner That Would Withstand Public Scrutiny*** — Imagine that any record in your agency, from a report on the expenditure of grant funds to an expense reimbursement request from the executive director, could be featured on a popular Web site or the subject of a story running in a local paper, at any time.

2. ***Stay Mission-Focused*** — Among the temptations facing nonprofit executives is the lure of generating an uninterrupted revenue stream from an activity that falls beyond the scope of the organization's mission or, at worst, calls into question the integrity of the organization or its managers. Remember the medical association that drew fire when it became the paid endorser of the products of a home health-care company. It is both possible and increasingly popular to spin off a subsidiary organization where unrelated-business income can be generated without jeopardizing the tax-exempt status of the parent nonprofit. Creating such a spinoff is a complex matter for which a nonprofit should obtain legal counsel. Outside this type of arrangement, a key to accountability is staying true to the nonprofit's mission.

3. ***Take the High Road with Staff and Volunteers*** — Although legally permissible in many instances, terminating staff on the spot and without notice (except in instances where gross misconduct has occurred) is rarely a good idea. Doing so damages morale among staff, who start feeling: "Maybe I'm next!" It also flies in the face of the compassion and caring most nonprofits require in their dealings with service recipients. Taking the high road means giving poor performers — paid *and* volunteer staff — time to adjust their performance to meet your expectations. For example, if an employee is failing to complete administrative paperwork on time and seems to be wasting time on the telephone or Internet, his supervisor should bring these matters to the employee's attention and request that improvement in both areas be made within a certain time frame. It is important to give staff enough time to demonstrate a change in behavior. If paperwork is due weekly, it would take several weeks to observe a marked improvement. Some offenses can be addressed immediately. For example, it would make sense to tell an employee that he must refrain from using profane language immediately. It would not make sense to give the employee 30 days to make this change. Taking the high road takes more time and effort, but it pays off in the long run when a nonprofit avoids a potentially time-consuming and costly administrative complaint or civil lawsuit alleging wrongful employment practices.

Vulnerable Clients

While *some* businesses specifically serve vulnerable populations and many encounter children, the elderly and persons with disabilities as occasional customers, *most* community-serving nonprofits are dedicated to serving a *vulnerable* client population. By *vulnerable*, we mean persons who are more likely to be mistreated due to their age, economic circumstances, or physical or mental heath. Vulnerable population groups include:

- Children

- Victims of domestic abuse

- Persons with alcohol or chemical dependency

- Elderly persons

- Persons with disabilities

- Homeless persons

- Poor working families

When a nonprofit sets outs to assist a vulnerable client group, it must recognize that it may be obligated to do more than "what it can" to help its clients. A heightened duty of care may apply. It must take specific steps to mind the safety and well-being of clients that it serves or risk liability for foreseeable harm that results from its operations. For example, the passenger in a wheelchair-equipped van is improperly assisted and falls from the lift, suffering a serious injury. Or a teenage resident at a rehabilitation clinic is not properly supervised, gains access to the roof of the building and jumps off the roof. Returning to the positive side of risk, a nonprofit that serves young people may be the beneficiary of a new community foundation dedicated to helping children. Or a local recreation program may receive an unexpected gift from a donor who specified that his assets be distributed among youth-serving organizations in the community.

To address the upside and downside risks inherent in serving members of a vulnerable population, a nonprofit should give special attention to the issues of screening, supervision, program design and clients.

1. ***Screening*** — A effective screening process increases the odds of making the right match between applicant and position, while reducing the chance that someone ill-suited for volunteer or employee status in the nonprofit will be hired. Therefore, screening is a tool for managing both upside and downside risks. Many nonprofits approach screening as a simple method of removing bad apples from the applicant mix. Unfortunately, it is not that simple.

Many organizations have adopted a uniform approach to screening for all positions. It is not hard to understand why. One screening process is far easier to manage than multiple processes that depend on the position at issue. Others feel that by subjecting all personnel to a rigorous screening process the organization sends the message that "we're all in this together," avoiding the possibility that some staff will feel that they have been treated unfairly. Yet a single process rarely works for a complex nonprofit. A process that includes rigorous elements, such as state-based criminal-history background checks, credit checks and home visits, is too invasive for many positions on the organization's payroll or volunteer roster. And a process that is too rudimentary, requiring, for example that only a résumé be submitted and one personal reference, may not be sufficient for certain moderate- and high-risk positions in an organization.

Using a screening process as part of an organization's strategic risk management approach for people-related risks requires the careful consideration of the following issues:

The *risk rating* of a specific position in your nonprofit may differ based on the assets in question. For example, a tutor position working with a group of adults in a public library may be rated as *low risk* where the safety of clients in the literacy program is concerned, but *moderate risk* when the tutor's responsibilities include taking cash donations to the bank each week.

❏ **Risk Assessment** — Though time consuming, a nonprofit should examine the positions in the organization and determine the relative risk of each position. This *risk assessment* of key positions is a starting point for determining the appropriate screening protocol. For example, certain positions, such as receptionist or meetings planner, may be graded *low risk*, because the positions do not involve one-on-one unsupervised contact with clients or money-handling responsibilities. Other positions may be graded *moderate risk*, because they require supervised client contact or advocacy of the nonprofit's interest with elected officials. A handful of positions may be labeled *high risk*, because they require unsupervised contact with children; these would include teachers, mentors, tutors, group-home staff and camp counselors. The results of this risk assessment based on position provide a blueprint for the approach to screening. The greater the risks posed by the position, the greater the focus on the screening process, both in terms of the type and quantity of tools that will be used.

❏ **Tools** — Every nonprofit must choose from a wide array of tools in designing its screening processes. From background checks and pre-employment tests, to references and home visits, tools should be carefully selected and uniformly administered to ensure their usefulness to the nonprofit while minimizing legal risk. As indicated, the scope of the screening process should reflect the risks in the vacant position: high-risk positions generally incorporate a greater number of screening tools, as well as those that might be considered invasive, such as requiring fingerprints to facilitate an FBI criminal-history background check. For more information on the types of tools available and their use in a nonprofit, consult the *Staff Screening Tool Kit: Building a Strong Foundation Through Careful Staffing*, a publication of the Nonprofit Risk Management Center.

❏ **Liability** — There are legal risks associated with staff screening. Two basic scenarios capture the legal risks of screening:

- the risk of not screening thoroughly enough, and

- the risk of violating an applicant's legal rights.

Risks associated with *not* screening candidates can be significant. The basic legal standard that applies to screening is *reasonableness under the circumstances*. If a nonprofit's screening process is challenged in court, a judge or jury will evaluate the reasonableness of the process employed; the foreseeability of the risk (whether the organization knew or should have known of the risk of harm); and whether the screening process, or lack of it, caused or contributed to the harm at issue.

For most nonprofits, a desire to match the most appropriate applicant with the position drives the design of the hiring process for the organization. Yet the fear of potential legal liability — not doing enough to check out the background of applicants — may be another significant motivator.

For most nonprofits, a desire to match the most appropriate applicant with the position drives the design of the hiring process for the organization. Yet the fear of potential legal liability — not doing enough to check out the background of applicants — may be another significant motivator.

Not Screening Thoroughly Enough — Under this scenario, the nonprofit faces a fraud loss after its newly appointed executive director depletes the reserve fund by writing checks payable to cash and the organization did not know of his history of embezzlement. Or major donors withdraw their support for the organization when they learn that the head of a child abuse prevention organization is a registered sex offender. Or a client of the nonprofit is victimized by a teacher, who has served time for assault and battery of clients of his previous employer. The potential plaintiffs under these scenarios are persons injured by the nonprofit's staff member who was arguably unfit for service. Liability is imposed when a court determines that the nonprofit should have known that the applicant posed an undue risk.

Violating the Applicant's Legal Rights — Under this scenario, the likely plaintiff is an applicant who was rejected by a nonprofit or who believes that personal information was disclosed to persons without a *need to know*. For example, a candidate who was not chosen sues the nonprofit after learning that the results of a negative reference check were circulated to the board of directors and staff of the organization.

There are no hard-and-fast legal rules about screening. Liability for negligent screening requires a thoughtful analysis of the circumstances.

2. ***Making Your Expectations Clear*** — Managers and board members of some nonprofits feel that an explicit statement prohibiting sexual acts with service recipients is unnecessary, because no one in their right mind would consider such relationships to be proper. Unfortunately, the prevalence of inappropriate sexual conduct involving staff members and vulnerable service recipients gives rise to the need to clearly state what should be obvious. By making these statements during the screening process, individuals who are seeking a position with your organization to gain access to sexual opportunities will be on notice that the organization *does not* and *will not* tolerate such behaviors. Applicants also need to know the organization's guidelines for discipline and control. If an applicant appears to be unwilling — or unable — to adapt to the organization's guidelines for exercising control over service recipients, the organization would be well advised not to place the applicant in a position that requires supervising activities for service recipients.

Code of Conduct — A growing number of organizations serving vulnerable populations have incorporated a written statement of expected behavior into their staff selection and screening process. If an applicant is unwilling to sign the statement of behavioral expectations, the organization rejects the application.

An orientation program is an important tool for reducing the risk that staff members will behave inappropriately toward clients or otherwise violate the organization's rules and procedures. An effective orientation provides a clear explanation of the organization's mission, policies, procedures and expectations, and affords an opportunity for participants to pose questions about specific circumstances. New staff members also need to know how to respond in situations in which the safety of service recipients is at stake. During the orientation session, their attention should be directed to policies that relate to first aid, emergency medical treatment, reporting to the organization, medical forms, and other information the organization should have on file about these service recipients.

New staff members need information concerning proper assistance techniques. For example, when assisting service recipients into and out of wheelchairs, they need to know how to set the brakes on the wheelchairs, how to place the footrests, where to hold the person, and how to lift without injuring the person being helped or the staff member. Keep in mind that vulnerable service recipients, both children and adults, may be targets for abuse. Staff members need to know what abuse is, how to detect abuse, what actions to take when abuse of a service recipient is suspected, and what the staff member's legal responsibilities are.

3. ***Program Design*** — Every nonprofit should periodically examine the programs and services it offers to determine if these services further the organization's mission. When the potential for harm to participants is high, a greater level of scrutiny should apply. An organization should only place the safety of its service recipients at risk to the degree necessary to accomplish its mission. Even then, the risks should be assessed and appropriate risk management strategies employed to lower the risks to an acceptable level.

    Activities and services offered by your organization to members of vulnerable populations should be examined for their appropriateness. Appropriateness may be measured in the context of the mental, physical and emotional requirements for the program. While it may be desirable to challenge participants to achieve more than they thought they could, it is counter-productive — and may be unsafe — to select activities that are inherently dangerous or have risks that cannot be reduced to a safe level due to limitations of your service recipients.

4. ***Participants*** — The managers of a nonprofit serving a particular client group, such as elderly residents of a small community, may believe that they fully understand the needs and characteristics of their client population. The organization may have been founded by an individual in the population group, a professional trained to assist the population group or the family member of someone in the population group. This orientation to its clients is a good foundation, yet it does not guarantee that personnel who join the organization's ranks in the future will have the same degree of preparedness. It is up to the nonprofit to make certain that incoming paid staff and volunteers develop an understanding of the population so that they can provide appropriate assistance.

Through a thorough orientation program, in-service training, and by reaching out to clients to evaluate their needs and concerns on an ongoing basis, an organization increases the odds that it will avoid accidents involving service to clients and take advantage of opportunities to provide meaningful assistance.

Transportation Programs

Transportation is the means for an organization to carry clients, volunteers, employees, goods, or equipment from one place to another. For many nonprofits, transportation services are an integral part of fulfilling the organization's charitable mission. For example, a nonprofit that delivers hot meals to shut-ins cannot operate without volunteers or employees driving either their own or agency vehicles. Many nonprofits that do not provide transportation services overlook their incidental transportation exposures. It is nearly impossible for a nonprofit to operate today and not have some form of transportation exposure. The risks may arise from *incidental driving* such as an employee or volunteer driving his or her own vehicle to attend meetings, or an agency function, or to run an errand to the bank, post office, or office supply store.

While every nonprofit has the possibility of a loss from an automobile claim, the level of risk increases when an organization's core business includes transporting people, materials, or equipment, or when an organization owns or leases vehicles. Therefore, your nonprofit should be diligent in managing the risks associated with your transportation activities, as well as the risks from incidental driving.

It is always prudent to consider whether your nonprofit's transportation activities are essential to achieving your core mission, or whether you can transfer or share the risk of loss by engaging a contract provider of transportation services.

Written Transportation Policies

Aside from appropriate insurance, every nonprofit should consider adopting a range of transportation policies that protect the organization, as well as the persons being transported as part of the nonprofit's programs.

Written policies and procedures concerning transportation activities are essential for any organization that provides transportation services as a major part of its operations or owns any vehicles. However, all nonprofits, even those with minimal transportation exposures (no agency-owned vehicles), should consider establishing a few basic written transportation policies and procedures.

If your nonprofit owns vehicles or provides transportation services, you should consider incorporating the following policies into your transportation program:

❑ *Transportation Risk Management Statement* — A Transportation Risk Management Statement expresses the nonprofit's risk management philosophy regarding transportation. The most basic statement is that safety always comes first and is the number one priority within the organization. You can also include your basic driver safety rules, such as always wear seatbelts, lock car doors, no loud music, and do not drive when tired or taking medication that impairs your abilities.

❑ *Authorized Drivers and Use of Vehicles* — This policy specifies who may and may not drive for the organization and is an important risk management tool. The policy may include a requirement that employees and volunteers notify your organization if they are charged with any serious traffic violation. Occurrences may include reckless driving, driving under the influence or while intoxicated, or an at-fault accident. You can also state that your organization has the right to withdraw, at any time, its authorization of any employee or volunteer to drive on agency business. The policy should also address any limitations or restrictions on the use of agency-owned vehicles or the use of personal cars on agency business.

❑ *Passenger Responsibilities* — If your nonprofit transports passengers, consider developing guidelines that passengers must follow when being transported by your personnel. For example, all passengers transported by your paid and volunteer staff should be required to use basic safety equipment such as seatbelts, child safety seats, and wheelchair tie-downs as needed. Passengers should also adhere to minimum safety procedures, such as not causing distractions to the driver of the vehicle, remaining seated, not playing loud music, and no rowdy behavior while in the vehicle. Drivers and other passengers should be required to report all violations of these rules to the appropriate personnel. Take action when passengers repeatedly violate the organization's rules, such as suspending future transportation privileges. Encourage passengers to report any observed unsafe driving practices to the appropriate personnel.

❑ *Accident and Incident Reporting* — Develop instructions on how to respond in the event of a motor vehicle accident and procedures for reporting an accident to your organization and, if appropriate, to your organization's insurance broker and insurance companies.

❑ *Driver Selection and Licensing* — Put your driver selection process in writing so that you can readily explain how your nonprofit selects and approves persons to drive on behalf of the organization. As a rule of thumb, the greater the transportation exposure, the more extensive the driver screening process should be. First, review each employee and volunteer position description to determine if driving is a part of the position. The extent of the transportation exposure will vary by the position. A basic screening process might include an application, personal interview, reference checks, verification that the applicant has a valid driver's license, and proof of personal auto insurance. Additional items that might be considered in a more rigorous process include a statement of driving history, statement of medical condition, motor vehicle record, and a driving test.

❑ *Driver Training and Supervision* — Risk management does not end with driver selection. Proper training and supervision is critical to an effective transportation risk management program.

❑ *Vehicle Use* — A vehicle use policy provides information on the authorized use of the agency's owned or leased vehicles including any use restrictions. For example:

- who is authorized to drive the agency's vehicles;

- who is authorized to drive their own vehicles on behalf of the organization;

- the approved uses for the vehicles (transporting clients, materials and equipment);

- if employees, volunteers, or clients can use the vehicles for personal errands. If yes, the process for requesting and granting permission for personal use of the organization's vehicles;

- if members of the employee's or volunteer's family can drive the organization's vehicles;

- whether your organization prohibits any uses such as transporting hazardous materials, carrying passengers in an open truck bed, participating in car rallies, or other activities;

- what driving restrictions apply, such as limited night driving, limits on the number of hours someone may drive in one day, or the requirement that drivers take periodic rest breaks.

❑ *Vehicle Selection* — Develop guidelines for the purchase, leasing, rental or use of vehicles. The guidelines may restrict the use of certain types of vehicles or establish safety equipment criteria for agency vehicles. For example, you may have specific criteria for selecting the type of vehicle(s) your organization needs to fulfill its mission — private passenger cars, minivans, vans, various types of trucks, or buses. Your criteria may include the type of safety equipment that must be installed, such as airbags, side impact features, anti-lock brakes, four-wheel or all-wheel drive, head restraints, large side mirrors, back up alarms and mirrors, cargo holders and special mechanical equipment such as lifts. Finally, your policy may indicate how often you will replace your vehicles, and whether replacement is dependent upon the vehicles' age, mileage or obsolescence.

❑ *Vehicle Maintenance* — Your vehicle maintenance policy establishes and explains your agency's vehicle inspection and maintenance program.

❑ *Rental Vehicles* — Establish your policy for who can rent vehicles and what types of vehicles. Specify what insurance, if any, should be purchased through the rental agreement, such as liability and physical damage coverage.

❑ *Borrowed Vehicles* — Similar to the policy for rental vehicles; however, there is generally no formal agreement between the vehicle owner and the borrower. Remember that *the insurance follows the vehicle* and if the vehicle is uninsured, your organization may be held responsible for any loss that occurs while your employee or volunteer is driving the vehicle.

❑ *Insurance Requirements* — For personnel using their own vehicles, the organization can establish minimum insurance requirements for personal auto insurance. The policy may also require that personnel provide proof of their own insurance annually and, if they are unable to provide proof, their authorization to drive will be revoked automatically. The policy might also address insurance requirements for contract transportation services and for agency-owned vehicles.

If you have only an incidental transportation exposure (occasional driving by employees and/or volunteers and no agency-owned vehicles) you might consider including the following policies just described:

- ■ Transportation Risk Management Statement

- ■ Authorized Drivers and Use of Vehicles

- ■ Passenger Responsibilities

- ■ Accident and Incident Reporting

- ■ Driver Selection and Authorization

- ■ Rental Vehicles

- ■ Borrowed Vehicles

- ■ Insurance Requirements

Summary

Critical aspects of nonprofit organizations that require special risk management consideration include the use of volunteers, fund-raising programs, resource constraints, once-in-a-lifetime events, serving many masters, the delivery of services to vulnerable clients, and transportation programs. In each case, there are various practical strategies available to a nonprofit that seeks to prevent the erosion of its valuable assets and strengthen its opportunities. Risk management techniques can be useful on both fronts. It is important to include in your risk management planning process those areas that are common to other organizations (both nonprofit and for-profit), while devoting special attention to those that reflect the unique circumstances or operations of your nonprofit.

Inspiring a Risk Management Culture in Your Nonprofit

C reating a risk management culture in your nonprofit organization is like investing your hard-earned dollars in an account guaranteed to yield handsome periodic dividends.

The dividends in this case include:

- staff that feel confident moving ahead with ambitious service delivery projects because they know that contingencies have been considered;

- clients who believe that they do not get lost in the crowd — the nonprofit cares about their personal safety;

- board members who have a high level of confidence in the staff, yet are interested and engaged in the organization-wide effort to examine upside and downside risks as the organization embraces change;

- insurance and financing providers who view the nonprofit as a valuable client; and

- staff throughout the organization who believe that the safety of the nonprofit's assets and resources — including its people — is an important, shared responsibility.

In Chapter 1 we indicated that the traditional approach to risk management has been limited to threats of accidental loss. As a result, risk management practiced in this traditional sense is too tactical and has little or nothing to do with the opportunities for gain facing a nonprofit or losses from sources other than accidents. As described in Chapter 1, our hope is that readers will consider a broader, *strategic risk management* view that seeks to:

- *counter all losses*, including accidents, events out of the nonprofit's immediate control, and from unfortunate business judgments, and

- *seize opportunities for gains* through organizational innovation and growth so that risk management, at its best, enables your nonprofit (or any organization) to "be all it can be."

If this is the course your nonprofit intends to take, then the risk management culture must nurture staff both to recognize potential dangers or losses, as well as to cultivate opportunities.

While there is no single formula for inspiring a risk management culture that is guaranteed to work in every setting and context, we have identified a series of steps as one path to getting started.

Step 1
Set up a Body of Customary Beliefs

A strategic risk management culture that embraces asset protection, safety and critical goals is a universal mindset and an all-encompassing approach that steeps your staff with responsibility for making and keeping their environment, as well as the organization's vital assets, safe. For the culture to take hold in your nonprofit, risk management activities must be considered worthwhile by the nonprofit's board of directors, the executive director or president, senior management and the people on the front lines of service delivery. While having a full-time risk manager who champions and coordinates strategic risk management and safety programs is desirable, it is out of the reach of most small- to mid-sized organizations and a good percentage of large nonprofits. And even when this position or department has been created, people at all levels of the nonprofit must be involved. For most nonprofits, the most economical, efficient and enjoyable way to instill safe practices into the organization is to make risk management everyone's responsibility. Once you infuse your organization with a strategic risk management culture, what was seen as a task becomes automatic behavior. You want an environment where you will never hear, "Risk management doesn't have anything to do with my job...I think our CFO is responsible." Those who have experienced the phenomenon agree that the time spent in educating and monitoring staff is well worth the investment in reduced accidents and injuries, and increased opportunities to fulfill the organization's ambitious mission.

Here's a suggested To Do list for accomplishing Step 1:

❑ Recruit participants to serve on a risk management committee for your nonprofit. Tap people from all levels on the organizational chart, including persons who have shown an interest or concern about some aspect of safety in your organization.

❑ Charge the committee with drafting risk management goals for presentation and approval by your board of directors. These goals might include broad statements about workplace safety and client well-being, but they may go beyond traditional safety areas and consider the nonprofit's fund-raising activities, reputation and competitive position among similar nonprofits seeking donor support.

❑ Charge the committee with developing a set of value statements (customary beliefs) for risk management. These statements might express the committee's view about the importance of organization-wide commitment to efforts to protect and preserve assets.

❑ Charge the committee with examining whether changes in organizational policy (including the employee handbook, position descriptions, operating manual) are required to reflect an organization-wide commitment to risk management.

❑ Task the committee with proposing a strategy for involving the board in reviewing the strategic risk management program. Will the committee provide a written report as part of the staff materials developed in advance of each meeting? Will a board member serve as a liaison to the committee and deliver its message to the board? Will the board be asked to examine governance risks and suggest action based on its use of the risk management process?

Step 2
Establish and Communicate Your Expectations

When taught effectively, the principles of risk management can become second nature to each person in your nonprofit. They will not be able to walk by an unsafe situation without correcting it or alerting the appropriate person. When a new project is proposed, the staff will raise questions about how the organization can increase the odds of success, while minimizing the chances of failure, looking carefully at the probability and magnitude of potential losses and potential gains. While it is the job of the risk management committee to examine a wide set of risks and identify priorities, you do not want to create an environment where the proverbial iceberg at the prow of the ship is overlooked, because "Icebergs were not listed on this year's risk management plan." When something comes up mid-stream or mid-year — threats *and* opportunities — those who observe it should be empowered to fix either the problem or to raise the issue and suggest a solution or, in the case of upside risks, suggest a way to capitalize on the opportunity. The same principle applies when a staff member or volunteer observes a policy being ignored or purposefully violated.

Some policies are generic, such as picking up and properly disposing of the pesky banana peel. Others are mission specific, such as making certain young staff and clients are not taken off into isolated one-on-one situations. Once the priority list has been established, decide the appropriate action you expect to be taken in each situation. Then make your expectations clear to everyone. Some people are already sensitized to correct unsafe situations. Perhaps they learned it at their mother's knee. Other people are not observant or these situations just are not on their personal radar screens. If you define what you mean, everyone has an equal chance of meeting expectations.

Step 3
Have the Courage to Take Risks

Practicing strategic risk management requires having the enlightened courage to take reasonable risks that significantly advance your mission. Consider:

- building risk-taking into job descriptions,

- adding risk-taking skills to your performance appraisal process,

- developing specific annual risk-management performance goals that encourage risk-taking,

- praising people when they take risks, and

- designing skill-building exercises to teach people to use their innovation and creativity.

Step 4
Teach 'em to Talk the Talk and Walk the Walk

To create a risk management culture, educate employees and volunteers:

- *Why risk management is important to your nonprofit.* Your personnel should know that risk management is more than buying insurance; it is about protecting vital assets the nonprofit needs to thrive, including its people, property, income and reputation.

- *Why their involvement is key to managing risk.* Like the dominos in the Domino Theory discussed in Chapter 4, a single wobbly component can disrupt the good work of the nonprofit at a minimum, and bring the program crashing to a halt at worst. It is never enough to simply tell personnel that they play a vital role; the organization must follow through by valuing the suggestions and issues raised by staff as part of the program.

Step 5
Consider Benchmarks and Rewards

A growing number of nonprofits have adopted safety and risk management benchmarks as a way of communicating the organization's risk management goals and targets both within and outside the organization. Consider whether benchmarks and/or a rewards system could be effective in gaining internal support for your risk management goals and objectives.

As your risk management culture takes hold, confidence on the part of many key stakeholders should increase, even as the organization moves in new directions, tackles challenging issues, and harnesses innovation to address difficult problems.

Glossary

This glossary is designed to be a reference for nonprofit managers and volunteers responsible for risk management. The definitions are applicable to the nonprofit sector. Although accurate, the definitions vary from those the reader might find in a legal dictionary or insurance textbook.

Accident — Unexpected or chance event.

Adaptation — Readiness to adjust to change that already is occurring or has occurred.

Appraising risks — A general term for estimating, evaluating, judging and/or setting priorities among the ways in which the future may be surprisingly different from what we expect it to be for our nonprofit.

Avoidance — Risk management strategy in which a nonprofit avoids an activity or service to reduce the probability of risk to zero.

Board of directors — Governance body of a nonprofit made up of individuals who are appointed or elected and whose function it is to provide policy, and sometimes management, direction for the purpose of accomplishing the organization's mission.

Breach of contract — A civil wrong growing out of a contractual relationship.

Bylaws — Set of rules that outline how a nonprofit organization operates, including rules describing key positions and their respective duties, election of officers, frequency of board meetings, and quorum requirements.

Care, Duty of — Standard of behavior required by a nonprofit board member or officer in making decisions. The standard is to use the level of care that a reasonably prudent person would exercise in a similar situation.

Casualty insurance — A category of insurance that offers protection against losses caused by injuries to persons or damage to property of others and the legal liability imposed on an insured for the injury or damage.

Cause of loss — The force that most directly or most predominantly brings about a loss.

Civil wrong — Wrongful action that causes harm to one or more specific individuals or organizations.

Criminal wrong — Wrongful acts that not only harm particular individuals or organizations but also endanger the community as a whole.

Danger — An action or a condition that tends to increase the probability or the magnitude of a loss.

Defendant — Individual or organization against whom a lawsuit has been brought.

Dimension — Ways in which risk arises because the future may surprise your nonprofit.

Donee — An individual or organization that receives a gift or donation.

Donor — An individual or organization that makes a gift, or donation, to an individual organization.

Fiscal year — The 12-month period in which the organization keeps its financial records and books.

Frequency — A measure of how often the risk is likely to materialize, or the probability of the risk materializing.

Fundraising — The process by which a nonprofit organization solicits and obtains donations (monetary, in-kind, or other categories) for general or specified purposes to enable it to achieve its mission.

Grant — The transfer of money or property from one entity, usually a charitable foundation or governmental entity, to another (either an individual or charitable organization), in the form of a contribution to enable the recipient to offer some service or charitable benefit.

Income — An organization's revenue, (grants, investment earnings, contributions, contract fees, fees for services, and revenue from the sale of goods).

Indemnify — A promise to reimbuse another for a loss suffered.

Innovation — A change in technology, operating procedures, products, marketing, or any other aspect of a nonprofit's activities, that its management actually creates — a new way doing something that is better than anyone has ever done it previously.

In-service — In-house training session for staff and volunteers.

Insurance — A contract whereby an organization agrees to indemnify another and to pay a specified amount upon determinable contingencies in exchange for a premium. A form of shared financial risk.

Liability — Any enforceable legal obligation.

Litigation — Describes the activities that emerge from a lawsuit or legal proceeding. The nonprofit receives a summons, and must defend itself in court.

Loyalty, Duty of — Standard of behavior that requires a director or officer (of a board) to pursue the interests of the organization, particularly financial, rather than his/her own or the interests of another person. To place the organization's interests ahead of his/her own.

Magnitude — Magnitude measures the cost (in positive or negative terms) should the risk materialize.

Minutes — Minutes are a summary and documentation of a board meeting. The specifications for acceptable minutes will vary with the organization, but should include who attended the meeting, the significant issues discussed, the actions taken on motions and resolutions, and reports of officers or committees.

Modification — Modification is a means of changing the activity so that the chance of harm occurring and impact of potential damage are within acceptable limits.

Negligence — Failure to take the legally required degree of care for the safety of another.

Nonprofit organization — An organization in which no part of its income is distributable to its members, directors, officers, stockholders or other individuals and that meets the state statute designation of a nonprofit entity. *Note:* while most people equate nonprofit organizations with charitable or 501(c)(3) entities (those that are eligible for receive tax-deductible contributions), other categories of nonprofits exist as well, including trade associations and labor unions. An organization need not be tax-exempt to be recognized and organized as a nonprofit under state law.

Nonprofit sector (also called independent sector, charitable sector, voluntary sector or tax-exempt sector) — A collection of organizations that are formally constituted, private (as opposed to governmental), serving some public purpose, self-governing, voluntary, and not-profit-distributing.

Obedience, Duty of — Standard of care that obligates a director or officer (of a board) to act in a manner that demonstrates faithfulness to the organization's mission and obeys all applicable laws, statutes and regulations.

Occupational accident — Accident to an employee that occurs within and arising out of the course of employment.

Officer — Individual who has a fiduciary (trustee) responsibility within a nonprofit. This individual can be a member of the organization's board, executive committee or an employee of the organization.

People — Category of nonprofit assets at risk that includes board members, volunteers, employees, clients, donors, and the general public.

Personal injury liability — Injury to a person or organization that arises out of incidences of libel, slander, invasion of privacy, false arrest or detention, malicious prosecution, or wrongful entry or eviction.

Personally liable — Liability that an individual assumes when he/she is directly involved in the occurrence and cannot defer the liability to another person or entity.

Plaintiff — Individual or organization that initiates a lawsuit to obtain a remedy for an injury.

Probability — The percentage of times a specified event is likely, but not certain, to occur in the future. For example, since a coin has two sides, the probability of heads on one coin flip is 50 percent. Since one of a pair of dice (a die) has six sides, the probability of rolling a 4 (or any other number from 1 to 6) in one roll of one die is 1/6, or 16.67 percent. Or, if we know from experience that 6,000 out of every 100,000 people who live to be 70 die before reaching 71, the probability of dying between ages 70 and 71 is 6,000/100,000 or 6 percent.

Property — Category of nonprofit assets at risk that includes real property (buildings, improvements and betterments), personal property (furniture, fixtures, valuable papers and records, equipment, and supplies) and intangible property (copyrights, business reputation and trademarks).

Prudent person rule — Legal rule that individuals are expected to act with the same degree of care that a reasonably prudent individual would demonstrate in a similar situation.

Reputation — An organization's goodwill, stature in the community, and the ability to raise funds and appeal to prospective volunteers.

Respondeat superior — Legal principle by which employers are held responsible for the actions of those they supervise. Literally, the *master* shall answer for the acts of his *servant*. In the context of volunteer organizations, the nonprofit is the *master* and the volunteers and employees are the *servants* working on the organization's behalf.

Retention — A tool or technique in risk management whereby the nonprofit accepts all or a portion of the risk and prepares for the consequences. A deductible on an insurance policy is a form of retention.

Risk — Risk is a measure of the possibility that the future may be surprisingly different from what we expect.

Risk evaluation and prioritization — A step in the risk management process that examines the possibility of each risk becoming reality and estimates its probable value to the nonprofit. Organizations should examine their records to determine the probability and magnitude of common risks.

Risk identification — The second step in the risk management process that identifies the risks that are relevant to the organization. Also: Risk appraisal.

Risk management — A discipline for dealing with uncertainty. (See Strategic Risk Management).

Risk management techniques — Strategies for analyzing risk (identification, measurement and assessment) and responding to risk (control, finance and communication).

Risk management process — The risk management process contains five steps: (1) Establish the risk management context, (2) Appraise risks, (3) Select risk management techniques, (4) Implement the chosen techniques, and (5) Monitor and modify the risk management techniques. The process can also be viewed as comprising two steps: analyzing risk, and responding to risk.

Risk modification — The means of changing an activity so that the chance of harm occurring and impact of potential damage are within acceptable limits.

Risk sharing — A risk management tool whereby an organization shares risk with another organization. Examples of risk sharing include mutual aid agreements with other nonprofits, purchasing insurance, and sharing responsibility for a risk with another through a contractual agreement. Traditionally, risk management literature has referred to this option as *transfer* because of the presumption that is possible to transfer risk to another party.

Safeguard — An act or condition that makes a *gain*, not a loss, larger or more likely.

Staff — Volunteers (unpaid) and employees (paid) who carry out the work of an organization.

Strategic risk management — Using an organization's resources and activities to counter potential losses and seize potential gains. Running a nonprofit as best you can so that it may fulfill its mission to the fullest in an uncertain future.

Tort — A *civil wrong* that does not grow out of a contractual relationship.

Uncertainty — Lack of knowledge or belief about something.

Vicarious liability — Liability imposed on a person or organization for the acts, errors or omissions of persons serving on its behalf. Vicarious liability can be imposed even if the individual or organization is not directly involved in the occurrence. The liability of one party is imputed to another.

Volunteer — Individual who freely provides services to an organization without compensation other than reimbursement for reasonable expenses.

Workers' compensation — Coverage that insures the employer's responsibilities for injuries, disability or death to persons in his/her employ, as prescribed by law.

Glossary Sources:

Gifis, Steven H., *Law Dictionary*, 4th Edition, Barron's, Hauppauge, N.Y., 1996

Gifis, Steven H., *Law Dictionary*, Barron's Educational Series, Inc., Woodbury, NY, 1975.

Hopkins, Bruce R., *Nonprofit Law Dictionary*, Wiley, New York, N.Y., 1994.

Lorimer, James, J. [et al.], *The Legal Environment of Insurance*, 4th edition, American Institute for Property and Liability Underwriters, [now known as American Institute for CPCU], Malvern, Pa., 1993.

Salamon, Lester M., *America's Nonprofit Sector: A Primer*, 2nd edition, Foundation Center, New York, N.Y., 1999.

Resources

Bernstein, Peter L., *Against the Gods: The Remarkable Story of Risk,* John Wiley & Sons, New York, N.Y., 1996.

Church, Frederic, C., *Avoiding Surprises*, Boston Risk Management Corporation, Boston, Mass., 1982.

Grose, Vernon, L., *Managing Risk: Systematic Loss Prevention for Executives*, Prentice-Hall, Inc., Englewood Cliffs, N.J., 1987.

Jackson, Peggy, M. et al, *Mission Accomplished: A Practical Guide to Risk Management for Nonprofits*, Nonprofit Risk Management Center, Washington, D.C., 1999.

Wolf, Thomas, *Managing a Nonprofit Organization in the Twenty-First Century*, Simon & Schuster, Inc., New York, N.Y., 1999.

Risk Management Web Sites

Through the Internet, you can access virtually the entire universe of strategic risk management. Here are a few general Web sites with which to start. You can search each of them for information on specific topics, learn about the periodicals, booklets, books, videos and other materials they provide, and link to other Web sites. Explore, enjoy, learn — enable your nonprofit to be all it can be.

American Society of Safety Engineers (www.asse.org) — The most inclusive general loss prevention organization, offering a variety of written and audio-visual resources for both safety professions and general business managers, plus links to more specialized sites.

International Risk Management Institute (www.irmi.com) — A commercial publishing and seminar-sponsoring organization for both general and specific risk control and risk financing topics.

National Safety Council (www.nsc.org) — A fine source of booklet, brochures, and other shorter publications and videos to help the general public understand specific hazards and practical safety measures in workplace, home, and highway settings.

Nonprofit CARES (www.nonprofitcares.org) — The access point for Nonprofit CARES, the Nonprofit Computer Assisted Risk Evaluation System developed by the Nonprofit Risk Management Center. CARES is software that walks the user through a self-assessment questionnaire. After completing the questionaire, users can print a comprehensive report containing specific recommendations.

Nonprofit Risk Management Center (www.nonprofitrisk.org) — The only Web site devoted exclusively to risk management resources for nonprofit organizations. Hosted by the Nonprofit Risk Management Center, the site offers informative articles, free factsheets, online tutorials, an "ask a question" feature that enables visitors to pose risk management questions to the Center's professional staff, and information on all of the free and affordable resources offered by the Center.

Public Risk Management Association (www.primacentral.org) — The professional society, and a source of practical publications and videos, for risk managers of cities, counties, and other governmental entities, many of which face risk management challenges similar to those confronting nonprofit organizations.

Risk and Insurance Management Society (www.rims.org) — The most inclusive professional society for risk managers in the United States and Canada, offering many general publications and videos that, although directed primarily to for-profit organizations, provide good information and strategies for all organizations, especially in risk financing.

Risk Management Resource Center (www.eriskcenter.org) — A Web site that merges the online resources of the Nonprofit Risk Management Center, the Public Risk Management Center and the Public Entity Risk Institute, enabling users to search all three sites simultaneously and to link to a very broad range of related organizations.

Publications Available from the
Nonprofit Risk Management Center
www.nonprofitrisk.org

Enlightened Risk Taking: The Workbook

This companion piece to *Enlightened Risk Taking* is essential if you are serious about launching a risk management program to safeguard against losses while seizing the opportunities for gain. *The Workbook* contains sample forms and checklists that will help you formulate a risk management program from scratch or expand a current program to incorporate recognizing and taking advantage of opportunities for gain. 2002 / 52 pages / **$15.00**

Coverage, Claims & Consequences: An Insurance Handbook for Nonprofits

Nonprofit organizations purchase insurance for many reasons, covering many exposures (risks), at a wide range of prices. This book puts insurance in perspective as a risk-financing tool that is part of an overall risk management strategy. When you've read this book, you'll have an overview of what insurance can and can't do to protect your nonprofit's mission. You'll understand the role of an insurance professional and how to go about evaluating the services you're receiving and putting your insurance program "out to bid." You'll be able to identify and rank the types of protection you would like to have and know how to go about reading and understanding insurance contracts. You'll understand why insurance is hard to obtain and costs more during some years and vice versa. Anyway you slice it; insurance is a complicated topic. This book helps cut through the confusion and unfamiliar terms, putting comprehensive insurance protection within reach for your nonprofit. 2002 / 218 pages / **$30.00**

The Season of Hope: A Risk Management Guide for Youth-Serving Nonprofits

The Season of Hope addresses an array of questions from youth-serving organizations about protecting children in a nonprofit's charge from harm, whether they are program participants, employees or volunteers. This new, comprehensive, practical book encompasses much of the material in the Center's well-received *Child Abuse Prevention Primer* and much, much more. Learn which risks are inherent in your program due to the developmental stage (infancy through adolescence) of the participants. Build your own plan from examples of risk management strategies for violence, health, injuries and accidents, and Internet access. Its broad focus approach speaks to youth development professionals, executive directors, board members, directors of volunteers and human resource managers. Adults in general can no longer ensure the safety of young people as they grow and develop, but they can mitigate the risks inherent in their youth-serving programs with help from *The Season of Hope*. 2002 / 156 pages / **$30.00**

Full Speed Ahead: Managing Technology Risk in the Nonprofit World

No matter how large or small your technological advances, they are critical to your mission. This book will help you protect your people, financial and property assets, whether you have two PCs networked together or a multisystem network at remote locations. *Full Speed Ahead* addresses how the wired and wireless worlds affect employment practices, staffing plans, volunteer recruitment, fundraising, crisis management, copyright, security, privacy and confidentiality, client protection and insurance coverage. 2001 / 122 pages / **$25.00**

No Surprises: Harmonizing Risk and Reward in Volunteer Management — *2nd Edition*

This second edition of the popular *No Surprises* is a clear, easy-to-read guide that demystifies risk management and explains this responsibility of every director of volunteers in any type of setting. Learn how to limit risk at each step of managing a volunteer program: in volunteer job design, the application and screening process, and ongoing training and supervision. This expanded edition includes privacy and technology risk reduction methods. 2001 / 95 pages / $15.00

No Strings Attached: Managing the Risks of Fundraising & Collaboration

This publication provides a practical framework through which nonprofit CEOs, boards, and others engaged in fund-raising can address the risks and pursue fundraising responsibly. The authors address the risks associated with budgeting, raising money from foundations, soliciting individual donors, obtaining corporate support, negotiating collaborations and partnerships, and the challenge of restricted funding. 1999 / 95 pages / $15.00

Taking the High Road: A Guide to Effective and Legal Employment Practices for Nonprofits

This book is the first comprehensive guide to employment risk management for nonprofits. You will learn how to do the right thing, comply with the law, and stay out of trouble. Topics addressed in the book include avoiding illegal discrimination, complying with the ADA, developing a CEO contract, updating an employee handbook, conducting drug testing, complying with family and medical leave laws and safe reference-giving practices. 1999 / 217 pages / $45.00

More Than a Matter of Trust: Managing the Risks of Mentoring

All social service programs face risks, but the elements of trust and personal relationships dramatically raise the stakes for mentoring programs. This book will help you develop a solid risk management plan for your mentoring program that will help you protect your mentees, your mentors and your organization's assets — including its good name. *More Than a Matter of Trust* explains the legal liabilities that mentoring programs face and shows you how to develop a risk management plan by presenting "10 Keys to Mentoring Risk Management." 1998 / 59 pages / $15.00

Staff Screening Tool Kit: Building a Strong Foundation Through Careful Staffing — *2nd Edition*

Several thousand nonprofit and other organizations have used the first edition of the *Staff Screening Tool Kit* for guidance on effective screening. Since the original *Tool Kit* was first published, changes have taken place that influence the screening process and govern access to records. Besides these issues, the second edition addresses the increased focus on official agency records as tools for staff screening, and features a state-by-state directory of agencies that maintain records useful for screening. 1998 / 135 pages / $30.00

To see a complete listing of available publications, visit www.nonprofit**risk**.org.

To place an order, visit our Web site or call (202) 785-3891, today.